THE
EVOLUTION
OF
RUSSIA

THE EVOLUTION OF RUSSIA

OTTO HOETZSCH

THAMES AND HUDSON · LONDON

Translated from the German by Rhys Evans

© THAMES AND HUDSON 1966
PRINTED IN GREAT BRITAIN BY JARROLD AND SONS LTD NORWICH

CONTENTS

This survey of Russian history aims to put the different periods in Russian development, from the beginnings in the ninth century to the establishment of the Soviet régime, into historical perspective and proportion. After half a century it is clear that the Revolution of 1917 was anything but a total break in continuity, and the more the historical foundations of the Soviet Union have become apparent, the more important has it become to determine how much still persists from earlier times. Both the Russian Empire before 1917 and the Soviet Union today, although the latter now includes millions of Asians and stretches over two-fifths of Asia, are in all essentials European communities, and there is no greater obstacle to a true understanding of Russian history than the view which treats it as an 'Asiatic state'. For this reason I have systematically compared developments and institutions in Russia with those in western Europe, seeking to show both the similarities and the differences. I have also placed special emphasis on social and economic developments. The greater the advances made by Russia, as an increasingly integrated nation in the material, technological and cultural spheres, the more necessary does it become for us not to limit our view to political events but to take account of social and economic developments and intellectual movements.

The Soviet Union today covers an area of almost nine million square miles, or one-sixth of the inhabited area of the earth. It is the largest self-contained state in the world, with a population of approximately 220 millions, made up of some 170 different nationalities. At the beginning of Russian history—that is, in the ninth and tenth centuries—it covered rather less than 150,000 square miles, comprising roughly sixteen of the provinces of Tsarist Russia, and was inhabited by the three components of the Russian race—the Little Russians (Ukrainians), the White Russians, and the Great (or colonial) Russians—which were later for many centuries to go their separate ways. These main tribes may have comprised half a million inhabitants in all. The state of Vladimir I (980–1015) must therefore have covered about one five-hundredth of the area of the Soviet Union today, and possessed about one four-hundredth of its population.

The territorial expansion of Russia was so vast a process that it is hard to find parallels in history. Neither the expansion of the Roman Empire nor that of the United States can compare with it in scale. It was a dominant factor in Russian history and it is therefore important to study its effects on the Russian people and to follow its course and consequences through the centuries. To begin with, Russia was a peripheral land, cut off from the heart of Europe. This fact largely accounts for the view that its character was essentially 'Asiatic'. In reality, the Russian peoples were from the beginning a branch of the European family. They belonged to the European group of the Indo-Germanic race, even though various Finno–Ugrian (i.e. Asiatic) elements were assimilated during the colonization of the north-east in the Middle Ages. And, as it developed, Russia became ever more closely involved with western Europe. At the same time its geographical situation forced it to wage constant war with Asia. The concept of Russia as Asiatic is therefore entirely misleading. Moreover, community with Europe was strengthened from about A D 1000 by the adoption of the Christian faith. The fact that this was East Roman, orthodox Christianity was always of consequence; but it never constituted an insuperable dividing-line between Russia and the West.

Geographically the Russian lands were divided between the great forests and the treeless area of the steppes. On the edge of the latter stood the city of Kiev with its famous Black Earth zone, beyond which the steppe extended southwards to the sea and away inland towards the south-east. Here, between the Ural mountains and the Black Sea, was the great gateway of the races through which, for centuries on end, the Asiatic peoples poured, destroying, subjecting and compelling the Russians to fight in defence. The contrast between the wooded zone and the region of the steppes left a deep

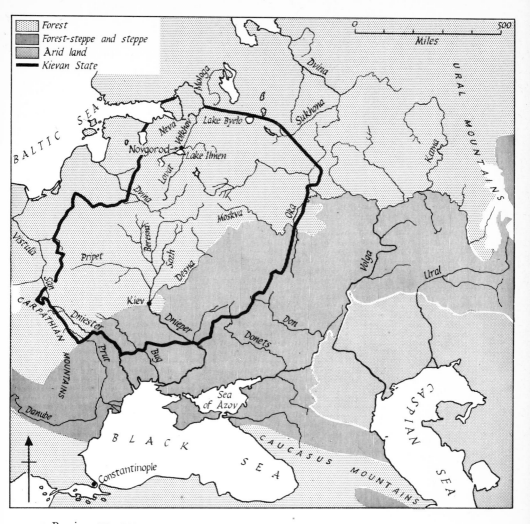

1 Russia *c.* AD 1000

9

impression on the character of the Russian people and their economy, which only modern technology has obliterated. It did not destroy the unity of the area, but it arrested its development. The system of rivers running from north to south—particularly the two great arteries, the Dnieper and the Volga—was an important factor in holding the country together. The prediction was often made that, as the population increased, the vast empire would collapse. But no single part could exist without the other: the wooded north required the grain-producing south; the industrial centre required both; the interior could not exist without the coast and without the great navigable waterway of the Volga.

As early as the ninth and tenth centuries the consciousness of underlying unity was expressed in the word *Rusi* as an appellation for the Russian people in all its branches. Not even such disasters as the Tartar invasions, or the later Napoleonic and German attacks, destroyed this sense of common Russian nationality. Under the Tsars, with their autocratic claims and Great Russian chauvinism, this nationalism often took on aggressive and expansionist forms. In the Soviet Union, particularly during the Second World War, it was the expression, for all racial groups concerned, of the vital feeling of devotion to the fatherland.

These basic factors, territory and race, tradition and history, exerted a lasting influence on the evolution of Russia, both as a state and as a community, from 862 to 1945. Did this evolutionary process differ in any fundamental way from that of the countries of western Europe, or was it just a question of timing? According to the great Russian historian Klyuchevsky, the same historical forces and elements were at work in Russian history as in the other European communities. In Russia, however, these forces did not operate with the same intensity, and they also interacted in different ways. For this reason, in Klyuchevsky's view, Russian society 'bears a stamp of its own, the life of its people moves at its own pace . . . and is dependent on different combinations of circumstances.'

Chernyshevsky's view was similar. 'Russian history', he said, 'is only comprehensible in relation to world-history; its distinctive features are merely a modification of forces present everywhere.'

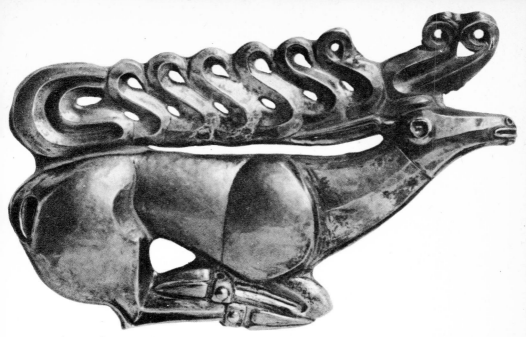

2 This Scythian carving in gold of a stag (seventh–sixth century B C) was found in a burial mound at Kostromskaya in the Kuban region of South Russia

Russia first emerges into the light of history in the sixth century A D. Only from then can we apply ordinary historical methods. Prior to that, there is a considerable quantity of archaeological material which casts some light on the early communities and their domiciles and wanderings, down to the time of the Scythians. Herodotus mentions their *kurgany* (burial mounds) along the central reaches of the Dnieper and the Don and the ancient Greek colonies on the Black Sea. The cultures of these early peoples, their migrations and institutions, are important though highly controversial subjects, and no less important are the early cultural contacts between Asia and Europe. But they belong to prehistory rather than to history, and cannot be discussed here. The study of language is also important, especially for the light it throws on the original domicile of the Slavs and the boundary between them and their neighbours in the north and east, the Finno-Ugrians. The linguistic evidence indicates that the latter were settled on the middle reaches of the Volga and

11

the Kama, and in the Urals, where remnants are still found today, though assimilated and mixed. By the time the east Slavs emerged into the light of day, the boundary between them and the Finno-Ugrians seems to have run south of the Neva, along the Mologa as far as the Moskva and the Oka. The Asiatic peoples who settled in southern Russia at a later date were, of course, different in origin. The Finno-Ugrians, on the other hand, were an important element in the colonization of north-eastern Russia.

The period following the emergence of the Slavs is also obscure. There is little doubt that at this time they were still organized in separate bands or tribes, and that it was the latter that carried out the settlement of the land. Their consolidation into a single body was gradual and slow, and was hardly completed before the dynasty of Rurik seized power. It was, indeed, with the Ruriks that the first phase of Russian, as opposed to tribal, history began. The Ruriks created a Russian state based on conquest and slavery, and conquest and slavery remained an essential feature of early Russian society up to the time of Vladimir I. Thereafter Russian history can be divided into four main periods: the Kiev period (980–1169); the first Moscow period (1169–1689); the Petersburg period (1689–1917); and the second Moscow period (1917 onwards). This scheme is, no doubt, in many ways superficial, and may give undue attention to the predominance of particular regions. Nevertheless the divisions are historically justified, and they help to give us a clear impression of the course of Russia's historical development as a whole, without forcing the important events and movements into an artificial mould.

3 Eleventh-century Swedish buckle from the region of Moscow, a relic of trade at the end of the Viking period

The two essential starting points in the history of Russia are the fusion of the east Slavs into tribes in the seventh century and the appearance in their midst in the ninth of the Normans and Vikings, Varangians as they were called by the Greeks, the Ruotsi as they were called by the Finns, or the Rusi as the east Slavs knew them.

We do not know how and when the Slavonic peoples became differentiated into west, east and south Slavs. In the fifth and sixth centuries AD, the east Slavs are mentioned in contemporary accounts; in the sixth century their existence between the Carpathians and the Dnieper becomes properly documented. From the seventh century onwards families and clans were first formed into tribes (*plemya*) under a prince who brought them to a higher level of social organization. They established settlements for the most part along river basins and were bound together by a tribal consciousness of a mythological and religious nature. Often they were on hostile terms with neighbouring tribes. This can be established from the well-known saga in the earliest chronicle which tells, under the year 862, of their appeal to the northern, non-Slav Varangians. 'Clan rose up against clan, and there was strife between them. Our land is great and rich, yet there is no order in it.' For this reason the appeal to the Varangians was made: 'Come, bring order to us and dispose over us.'

Among the principal tribes were the Polyane—around Kiev—and farther north the Drevlyane, both situated on the Dnieper; northwards from there were the Dregovichi on the river Pripyat; westwards were the Volynyane or Duleti on the western reaches of the river Bug, and the Chorvati along the Carpathians; southwards were the Tivertsi and the Ulichi in the eastern regions of the Bug, the Prut and the Dniester; there were also the Severayane on the river Desna, and then, farther north, the Radinichi on the river Sozh, the Polochani in the western parts of the Dvina, the Krivichi on the Lovat and on both sides of the Dnieper, and the Slovenians or Ilmen Slavs around Lake Ilmen and on the Volkhov. Eastwards, the

13

4, 5, 6 A brooch from Maikop in the Caucasus (*above*) shows a Sarmatian flourishing the head of a fallen opponent. Scythian warriors (*centre*) drink from the same horn in a ceremony of blood-brotherhood on this gold plaque from Kul Oba in the Crimea. The portrait of a Hunnic warrior (*right*) is a fragment of embroidery from Noin Ula in Mongolia

farthest removed of all were the Viatichi on the Oka. It is true that this division into tribes disappears completely from Russian history at an early stage, and never plays the part ascribed to Franks, Saxons, Bavarians and Swabians in German history. In this respect there is an enormous difference between the two; Russia never knew the tribal separation characteristic of Germany. Even the later division into Ukrainians, White Russians and Great Russians never acquired parallel importance.

Into the area inhabited by the tribes already mentioned other races also penetrated: the Scythians (from the seventh to the third centuries BC); the Sarmatians (in the second and third centuries AD); the Alans, a tribe of east German Goths (their dominion on the Dnieper under Ermanarich ended in 375); the Huns (from 372 until the second half of the fifth century); and the Avars (eighth century). They were followed by the chain of Asiatic races against which the Russians of the Kiev and Moscow periods had to struggle so hard for centuries. These migrations left no lasting traces. Despite the devastation they caused, it was during this period that the east Slavs completed the transition from hunting and fishing to agriculture and permanent settlement.

The encounter with the Varangians, from the ninth century onwards, was another matter. At that time the east Slavs were still engaged in primitive agriculture and the clearing of forest land. The Varangians were seafaring people, pirates and traders at the same time. They were warlike trading fraternities who boldly pursued old and new trade-routes, including the one across Russia which contemporary authorities call the route 'from the Varangians to the Greeks'. It led from the Dvina to the Dnieper and thence to the Black Sea and Constantinople, taking the rapids in its stride. The proximity of the sources of the rivers of north and south Russia facilitated this ancient and extremely significant trading activity.

For a long time there has been disagreement, mainly on nationalistic grounds, about the provenance of the Varangians, and above all as to whether they were Germanic or Slav in origin. The latter has been supported for the most part by Ukrainian historians; the former was and still is the opinion of most German and Russian scholars. There is no doubt that, in fact, they were Germanic. They were certainly not called in by the east Slavs, but came of their own accord both to subjugate and to ply their trade. It was almost certainly they who first laid the foundations of an east Slav state, or

at least who hastened the growth of one which was already in the process of development. But it is absurd to suppose that they appeared in
such large numbers that they completely Germanized the region, or
that its institutions and culture derived from them. There were far
too few of them for this; and these few were quickly absorbed into
the Russian environment which was already developing. Even so,
they left many traces behind them—for example, in the figures of
certain rulers who were indubitably Scandinavian; in a variety of
words and names; above all in paving the way for trading activities,
which had important effects on the class structure and the growth of
towns; and, finally, in various legal concepts and institutions. Particularly significant among the latter was the *druzhina* which the
Varangians introduced—i.e. the bodyguard on which the military
supremacy of the rising princely power was based. The *druzhina*
formed the basis of what was subsequently to become the boyar
nobility.

7 A duke and his *druzhina* riding in pursuit of SS. Boris and Gleb, younger sons
of Vladimir I who were murdered in a purge by an elder brother. Their canoniza-
tion, the first in Russia, discouraged speculation about their fate

8 The medieval kremlin ('fortress') and outer defences of Novgorod, showing traces of the earlier *vallum* of logs and stones bound with clay and originally surmounted by a log palisade

In the north, Novgorod was founded on Lake Ilmen, allegedly by Rurik in 862, as a trading centre and as the first political capital. Kiev had been founded some time previously, and in the second half of the ninth century it expanded and overshadowed Novgorod. Here, there appeared the figure of Prince Oleg (d. 912) who bound north and south more closely together. The centre of the new state lay on the Dnieper north of the rapids, but its line of expansion was southwards towards Constantinople. In 907, Oleg travelled thither, and as early as 912 he is said to have concluded a trading agreement with Byzantium. 'Russia was born on the route between two seas', and foreign trade was, from the beginning, a major factor in its rise. Thus the cradle of the new realm was in the south-west, on the left bank of the Dnieper, in the so-called Ukraine—a term meaning 'marchland' or 'frontier'. From the end of the ninth century, thanks to its propitious situation, Kiev became 'the mother of all Russian towns' and the centre of the first Russian state.

It was Vladimir I (980–1015) who first, by force and conquest, created a state out of the tribal regions. He was one of those rulers who, like Alexander the Great, Charlemagne or Boleslav Chrobry of Poland, were imbued with the conception of a vast political dominion, and managed by force and guile to unite a remarkably extensive territory, which soon collapsed because it lacked the necessary technical apparatus and communications. Although his personality is not so clearly delineated, Vladimir appears to posterity in much the same light as Charlemagne, and his achievements were similar.

9 Olga, the grandmother of Vladimir I, was an early noble Kievan convert to Christianity. This miniature shows her at the Byzantine court, where she received instruction in the middle of the tenth century

He envisaged a political structure far in advance of his time, and sought to displace the traditional society of family, clan and tribe by a real state, consolidated by force and subjugation. From the centre in Kiev and the middle reaches of the Dnieper, he spread his net westwards to the Prut, the San and the Carpathians, north-east to the Moskva and the source of the Don; northwards as far as Lake Byelo, Lake Ilmen, the western Dvina and the region of Novgorod; and southwards at least as far as the rapids of the Dnieper, which the traders of Kiev managed, in his day, to navigate down to the Black Sea and thence to Constantinople. His permanent bequest to his people was his concept of the political unity of the Russian lands, and this was reinforced by new ideological bonds when, in 988, he compelled them to accept Christianity in its Greek Orthodox form.

Like other great early empires which rose rapidly, Vladimir's soon collapsed. As in the Carolingian state in the ninth century, so in

18

eleventh-century Russia, brother struggled against brother over the inheritance which was treated as the private property of the ruling family. At the head stood the eldest member of the dynasty with the title of 'Grand Duke' (*vyeliky knyaz*) and his residence in Kiev. If he died it was not his eldest son who succeeded him, but the oldest surviving member of the family. This was the rule of 'seniority' which proved as fatal as in Poland. It was recognized in theory that the unity of the family ought to be maintained, but only rarely in the period of the principalities (*udely*), which began with Vladimir's death, was the power and authority of the Grand Duke sufficient to maintain unity and strength. The individual princes to whom parts of the realm had been allotted in their father's will, established themselves in their appanages and pursued policies of their own, often in opposition to the Grand Duke and to Kiev. So the internal situation fluctuated: Yaroslav I (1019–54) and later Vladimir Monomakh (1113–25) managed to consolidate their positions, but internal conflicts between princes undid their work.

10 The baptism of a Russian, presumably Vladimir, by the Patriarch of Constantinople, in a miniature from the Manasses Codex of 1345

ε †ελ̓γ οϲι το̄ῥϙμα τ·ῤμ̓ε ϊ·κ̔ μαικρου το̄ϕ ω̄τϊσα
δν̓ἀλσι· κω̄λ·ʒαν̄τ̓ϊΝο̄μ̓ο̄ΝομΔ ϊ̄̓κ̔π̄̄ μπ̄τ̄ τ̄ω̄
ἑ λ̓αχμικρω̄ ·τρἐ̓ιβεϊϲ

11, 12 Vladimir, converted about 990, was the first Russian prince to accept Christianity. The miniature above shows his envoys visiting the court of Emperor Constantine IX and (right) arriving back at Kiev. He was soon venerated as a saint, as in the medieval painted banner (right) from Novgorod

13 The first Russian ruler to mint his own coins, Vladimir had them stamped with his portrait and crest (above)

14 Kievan cavalry invading Bulgaria under St Vladimir's father, Svyatoslav I (at centre, brandishing his sword), *c.* 971. The Bulgarians flee, leaving their dismembered dead

At the same time as the power of the Grand Duke was being undermined from within, it was assailed by invaders from the Mongolian steppes. These were the Khazars, Pechenegs and Polovtsians who are repeatedly mentioned in the chronicles: tribes of horsemen who ravaged the treeless regions of the south Russian steppe without hindrance. Against their onslaught and their devastation the Kievan state proved powerless.

It was this situation that brought the Kiev period to an end. In order to protect themselves against the invaders, the rulers of the principalities moved into the remoter forest regions and stayed away from Kiev. It was characteristic that when Andrey Bogolyubsky, prince of Suzdal, attacked and destroyed the city in 1169, he made no attempt to occupy it himself. His base lay east of Moscow in the Suzdal–Vladimir–Rostov region, between the middle and upper reaches of the Oka and the Volga, in the forest lands far away from the old trade-route 'from the Varangians to the Greeks'. At the same time there was a substantial movement of the population into the

22

15 Svyatoslav II (the Wise),
Grand Duke of Kiev,
and his family

16 Four of the five daughters of Yaroslav I. The three eldest became the queens of Harold Hardrada of Norway, Henry II of France and Andrew I of Hungary

wooded regions of the north-east. Clearing the forest as they went, they pressed on towards a new kind of life which was hard but safer than before. This colonization, which began around 1100 and lasted till 1300, played a major part in shaping the course of Russian history. In many ways parallel to German colonization in the period 1150–1350, it marked the beginning of the Muscovite state.

With this change in the centre of gravity the power of Kiev collapsed. The regions of Halich (later to be called Galicia) and Volhynia in the west secured independence, and this area, known as 'Red Russia', became for centuries a shuttlecock contended for by Russia, Lithuania and Poland; it was not finally re-attached to the mother country until 1945. In the north, Novgorod also reasserted its independence, developing its democratic and republican institutions, its contacts with Hanseatic trade and its vast colonial possessions stretching far up into the north and north-east. Kiev itself was conquered by the Tartars in 1240. It never again recovered its political importance, though it remained a commercial centre. It also remained, far more than Moscow, the spiritual, religious and ecclesiastical centre for a long time to come. Nevertheless by the end of the twelfth century the Kiev period had come to a close.

Hunting, fishing and forestry were the basis of everyday life for the thinly scattered population in this period. They also engaged in agriculture, though it is hotly disputed whether its basis, as once thought, was the cultivation of the common lands of the village community (*mir*, or, to use the official term, *obshchina*). At the same time, from the very beginning of the Kiev period, towns were in evidence. They had arisen at suitable points along the rivers, and their development was furthered by the bands of traders and warriors who carried on overseas trade with Byzantium in honey, wax, furs and even wood, which they collected or exacted as tribute from the subjugated population. The towns with their wooden fortifications were also places to which the rural population could flee in time of war. Kiev was by far the most important of them, and even at this early date Russia had active urban communities, which soon took pride in their buildings. But as yet, there were no town charters, and no separate class of townspeople or *bourgeoisie*.

17 Yaroslav's sarcophagus, 1054, in St Sophia, Kiev, is a striking example of Byzantine decoration

During the winter months produce was exacted by the prince and his following from the country population, and a large quantity of wares accumulated in Kiev. In the spring it was carried down the Dnieper, unloaded and reloaded at the rapids, where today the huge power station of Dnieprostroy stands, and was finally bartered in Constantinople, partly in exchange for other goods, partly for money. Commercial treaties regulated the trade. The Russians often stayed six months in Constantinople, and already had a considerable permanent trading organization there. In spite of its importance, however, this trading activity was only incidental to the primitive agriculture which was still prevalent.

We can nevertheless trace back to this period the first signs of a class structure which was to be of the greatest importance for the future. Between 850 and 1200 the old tribal organization gave way to a stratified society at the head of which stood the military caste, or *druzhina*, i.e. the warlike Varangian soldiers and traders, originally Vikings who soon became Slavs. Lower down the scale came the merchants (*kuptsy*), neither members of the *druzhina* nor a separate class, followed by the artisans in the towns. These were all free men. Then came the rural population: free peasants and hired workers. The lowest stratum in the social pyramid was represented by the slaves. The institution of slavery was unquestioned in Russia as else-

18 Gold cloisonné enamel pendant, with motifs of Persian origin, made at Kiev in the eleventh or twelfth century

19 St Sophia, Kiev, as it appeared in the eleventh century, the first great Russian structure in the Byzantine style (reconstruction)

where in ancient times. The Varangians were slave-owners and slave-traders, and the slaves were regarded as chattels. Thus, although no opposing classes had actually developed, there was a division as early as the Kiev period between the ruling, land-owning warriors and the labourers. This division foreshadowed later feudal society. Together with slavery, it was the basis of the social order, and it is clearly reflected in the code of Russian law (*Russkaya Pravda*) which was compiled between the eleventh and thirteenth centuries.

All the same, Kievan Russia was not essentially an absolutist or despotic state. Democratic elements are discernible in the gatherings of the tribal elders (comparable with the Germanic *Thing*) and of the townsfolk (*vyeche*), which originally administered and enforced the law. But at an early stage the power of the prince, supported by

27

his following, was superimposed. Often the princes appropriated all the power and assumed full control. Elsewhere their position was less secure, and in certain places, such as Novgorod, they shared power with the democratic elements. Nevertheless it was often possible for a powerful family to raise itself up above the others, to conquer, subdue and plunder, exact payments and rule through governors, military officials, judges and tax-gatherers.

These features were already present in a rudimentary form in the Kiev period. Strong personalities such as Vladimir I (980–1015) or Yaroslav I (1018–54) managed to strengthen this princely power (*knyaz*) in association with their *druzhina*. But that power was quickly weakened when, as often happened, quarrels broke out within the princely family. Its members regarded the realm as their private property, to be exploited and divided arbitrarily, like all other property. In the Kiev region, in particular, the dividing-up of the inheritance led to havoc. The dominant princely family nevertheless claimed the right to defend all the lands and provinces. It was driven by the desire for dominance and political power, which it asserted by aggression both in the east and the west. It possessed a primitive army, whose deeds of heroism were told in the poetry of the people. It embodied, in short, the notion of the state which it had already conveyed to the east Slavs.

Side by side with the institutions introduced by the Varangians, Christianity played a considerable part in the consolidation of the idea of a state. For Vladimir the main motive for the adoption of Christianity was the strengthening of his power through contact with Byzantium and through the Byzantine concept of the absolute ruler, instituted by God, to whom the Church with its divine authority was no more than a support and a servant. The adoption of Christianity by Vladimir exerted an enormous influence on the development of Russia right down to 1917. The Orthodox Church, which broke away from the Roman Church in 1054, introduced into eastern Europe not only the Christian faith but also the civilization, education and art that had grown up in Byzantium: it also introduced the Cyrillic script which, with certain simplifications, is the basis

of the Russian script of today. It is true that it divided Russia from

20 The Golden Gate at Vladimir. The main block, surmounted by a chapel, was built in 1164 by Andrey Bogolyubsky in the style of the great Kievan gate of Yaroslav I— itself an imitation of a Byzantine original. The bastions are of the eighteenth century

western Christendom by its liturgical forms and the peculiarities of its faith, and so contributed to its isolation; but at the same time it bound Russia to one of the great religions of the world. Instead of remaining heathen, the Russians became European Christians. In their worst moments of division and suppression, at the time of Tartar domination, the Church kept alive in them the consciousness of unity, which was embodied in the office of Metropolitan. Hence it is fair to say, with Masaryk, that 'the unity and centralization of the Russian lands is in origin due to the work of the Church'.

The Kiev period closed towards the end of the twelfth century, though many features of later periods can be traced back to it. As yet there was no question of firmly established institutions and attitudes. Only four of the princes mentioned in the sources can be accurately portrayed, and we know even less of the character of the ordinary Russian. The loose, cumbersome political structure, which had gradually been constructed around the prince between the ninth and twelfth centuries, was not destined to be permanent. The main reasons were the domestic struggles resulting from a wholly inadequate political constitution, the invasions of Asiatic peoples, the Lithuanian, German and Swedish attacks which were now beginning, and 29 the crusades which, by establishing direct contact between the West and the Orient, led to the collapse of the trade along the Dnieper to Constantinople. The political centre of gravity, and the population centres, shifted to the north-east. In place of the semi-urban Russia of the Kiev period, there now grew up in the back-woods a feudal Russia of landowners and villages. Thus began another epoch, in completely different geographical circumstances, and on a different economic basis.

But in addition to the basic economic, social, political and cultural institutions, which the colonists and princes took with them to the north-east, the consciousness of unity established in the Kiev period also remained alive. It was expressed in the concepts *Rusi*, the Russian land (*zyemlya*), the Russian people, in the language, the Church, the faith, in the *Russkaya Pravda*; it was expressed in poetry—for example, in the famous *Lay of Igor's Campaign*—in the oldest chronicle (the so-called Nestor chronicle), and in the feeling of dynastic unity binding together the descendants of Rurik. The population was so sparse, the area so great, and the level of culture so low that this could hardly as yet be called national unity. But its development was under way, and it was never again called in question, though its character changed during the great migration to the north-east and in the course of the first Moscow period.

21 The scholars who, under Svyatoslav II's patronage, made a collection of Biblical texts are shown in a miniature from the Svyatoslav Codex, 1073

This period saw the formation of the basic economic, social, political and cultural elements which shaped Russia until the Revolution of 1917. They distinguished it sharply from western Europe and isolated it in spite of European influences. Up to the death of Ivan IV in 1584 this period was marked by the colonization of the north-east, confusion and strife amongst the princes, political weakness, and domination by the Tartars. But it was also the time of the 'reassembly of the Russian lands' and of the development from feudalism and serfdom to absolutism and Tsarism. At the same time there was a great expansion of the Russian frontiers. The century between the death of Ivan IV (1584) and the beginning of the reign of Peter the Great (1682) represented a period of transition. After the 'Time of Troubles' (1584–1613) power was seized by the Romanovs, who held sway until the collapse of Tsarism in 1917.

THE PERIOD OF THE PRINCIPALITIES AND THE RISE OF MOSCOW (1169–1462)

The great spontaneous movement of colonization, which took place roughly between 1100 and 1300, dominated the first part of this period. 'Russia', the great Russian historian Klyuchevsky once said, 'is a land which calls for colonization.' His statement is still true. In the period under discussion, one wave of settlers followed another, first towards the north-east, then farther east across the Volga, then south-east to the Kuban region and to the Caspian Sea, and finally to Siberia, where the colonizing wave is still active today. Thus Russia is a colonial country in the same way as North America, and there are remarkable similarities between the 'winning of the West' and the Russian colonization of the north-east.

The motive behind this movement, which over-ran the Kaluga and Orel regions, was not the lust for conquest, trade, precious metals

22, 23 Peasants dancing, a rare image from medieval Russia of pleasures other than holy,

and the like, nor was it the direct result of lust for land; rather, it represented a desire for safety from oppression, from the interminable wars between the princes, and above all from the attacks and devastation wrought by the invaders who had occupied the steppes. The population withdrew to the inaccessible forest regions in the upper reaches of the Oka and the Volga, where at least they would be spared these troubles. At first this happened spontaneously; later settlers were attracted by the princes who had by then established urban centres in the newly colonized areas.

They were already inhabited by a sparse native Slav population, living in the unwooded river-basins. As a result of the colonizing movement between the twelfth and fourteenth centuries this native population was considerably strengthened. The colonists also encountered a population of hunters and fishermen of Finno-Ugrian (i.e. Asiatic) origin, but the sources report no conflict between them. Rather, the immigrants forced back the indigenous population and assimilated them peaceably. No doubt there was a mixture of races, but they did not become Asiatic; on the contrary, it would appear that the Slavs gained full ascendancy over the native element.

It is impossible to determine exactly how the immigrants carried out the settlement of these wild forest regions. But it is reasonable to assume, as the colonization of Siberia in the nineteenth and twen-

32

and woodcutters clearing the land in the Novgorod district, in the eleventh century

tieth centuries would indicate, that it was done on a communal basis. One or more families, co-operating in forest clearance, charcoal-burning and open-field rotation, probably held the newly acquired terrain collectively. This was most likely the origin of the Great Russian *mir*, or peasant community, which corresponds closely to the German *Marktgenossenschaft*. The individual had his house, farm and garden, but the main source of production, the open fields in which each individual shared, were the collective property of the village commune. They were subject to periodical redistributions, but the individual had to obey the compulsory rules of common farming. Some such organization was in existence at the time of the colonization. Later it became more complex and unwieldy; but it was so deeply ingrained that it lasted until 1906, and was only finally superseded by the *kolkhoz* (collective farm) organization of today.

Colonization increased enormously the areas held by the east Slavs. It carried them to the Donets and across the upper reaches of the Oka to the Volga; in the north they were extended almost as far as the Sukhona. No less important, by increasing the population in the north, it consolidated the power of the princes who were busy establishing their hold in those areas. This was the period of the principalities. It lasted from the beginning of the eleventh century to 1523, but the decisive phase fell in the thirteenth and fourteenth

33

24 Mailed knights kneel
in adoration of an ikon
of the Virgin

25 Genghis Khan receives the homage of the men of Bokhara.
Of the the desolation which reached Moscow
a few years later it was written that
'The Churches mourned for their brethren . . .
as a mother mourns for her children.'

centuries. It was a period of confused struggles between individual branches or members of the Rurik dynasty, which undermined the power of the state. The Grand Dukes still ruled, but they were shadowy figures and their authority no longer extended over the whole of Russia. The principalities lay around Kiev, juxtaposed but without cohesion. They included Halich on the Dniester and Volhyn on the Bug; Novgorod was more isolated still; then there were Polotsk on the Beresina, Dvina, Smolensk, Chernigov, Novgorod-Severski and Pereyaslavl extending to the Donets; and finally the north-eastern group of Rostov, Ryazan, Murom, Vladimir–Suzdal, Tver and Moscow.

From around 1200 the Mongols (commonly but less accurately called the Tartars) began to penetrate this amorphous state. After

the battle of the Kalka in 1223 they ruled Russia until 1380 at least, and to a certain extent until 1480. Their rule, which lasted for some two and a half centuries, was not exerted directly but imposed from a distance. The seat of the Golden Horde, their central army head-quarters, was far to the east in Saray, near to Tsaritsyn (subsequently Stalingrad and now Volgograd) on the lower reaches of the Volga. From there, they were able to keep the people in subjugation for centuries on end, just as the Turks were later to do from Con-stantinople. The consequences of the period of Tartar rule have always been a matter of dispute. There are those who equate Russians with Tartars, echoing the famous saying coined by Napoleon or Mme de Staël: 'Scratch a Russian, and you will find a Tartar.' In reality, Mongol rule amounted to a heavy exaction of tribute, carried

26 Men of Vladimir-Suzdal advance to do battle with the Novgorodians and their guardian angel, a detail of a fifteenth-century ikon

out by the overseers and tax-collectors of the Khan. The Russians, both princes and people, were so weak that they were unable to shake themselves free of this yoke. The peasants and townsfolk paid the tribute. The princes also paid to have their status confirmed and went to the Khan's court to settle their quarrels. It was a long-lasting, enforced paralysis, similar to that which so long afflicted the Serbians, Greeks, Arabs and Egyptians in the Ottoman Empire.

There is no doubt that this situation, lasting as it did for over eight generations, deeply influenced the character both of the Russian people and of the Russian state. But it would be a definite exaggeration to speak of a 'Tartarization' of the Russian people. Very little Mongol blood penetrated into Russian veins. The Mongols did not interfere with the private life of the conquered people, with their administrative or legal systems, or with their religious life. They exerted no permanent cultural influence because their own cultural level was very low. The period of Mongol oppression had nevertheless two profound and lasting effects. In the first place the cruel, deceitful and degrading behaviour of the barbarian rulers, especially their contempt for human dignity, corrupted moral standards, particularly among the Russian princes, and the demoralization widened the breach between Russia and the European West. The second effect lay in the political sphere. Paradoxically, it was the necessity to pay tribute that held the tottering state together, integrating it at first unwillingly but then with the co-operation of the ambitious Grand Dukes of Moscow. Ivan I Kalita (1328–40) was the real founder of the Muscovite state. He received from the Khan, for himself and his descendants, the right to collect the tribute. He was responsible to the Khan for its payment, but, in return, he was able to exercise over his own subjects the Khan's unlimited power. This was, without doubt, an important factor in the development of absolute rule in Moscow, of despotism, autocracy and Tsardom. It marked a complete break with the function of the Grand Duke as conceived in the Kiev period.

27 Muscovy (left centre) as it appears on a map of 1516. The name 'Russia' is reserved by the cartographer for old Kievan Rus in the south

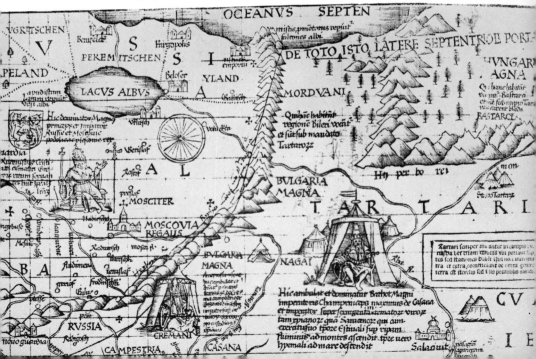

At the same time this weak, dependent state was exposed to attack from both north and west. In the north the Germans and Danes set up a barrier excluding it from the Baltic (in 1202 and 1237). On its western frontier, the Lithuanians, expanding far beyond their own territory, set out to establish a vast realm extending south to the Black Sea and taking in what was later called western Russia and the Dnieper basin. Grand Duke Vitovt (1392–1430) was an outstanding exponent of this Lithuanian policy. After the union of Lithuania and Poland in 1386, pressure from the west increased greatly. The struggle between the Lithuanian-Polish kingdom and Moscow for the western region round Smolensk and for the Ukraine continued for centuries and it was only in 1945 that this region finally came under Russian rule. In the fifteenth century, at the beginning of the Muscovite period, it seemed as though the Russian state, divided among the princes and dominated by the Mongols, had fallen into a hopeless coma, and was being driven back upon Asia.

28 Ivan *Kalita* ('Moneybags'), Grand Duke of Vladimir, Prince of Moscow and, as this sixteenth-century miniature shows, the Khan's energetic tax-farmer

ПОИМⸯ ЕРАТПАСВОЁ ІСНЅА ВОЛОДИМЕРА ІЙДЕ ИМИТРО ПО

И ПОВѢ'ДАЕМУ КА͠КО ШГН РАДЪ ІТПО ВСІКІН И Ш ЕРА

29 Dmitri Donskoi
setting out on a
campaign against
the Tartars which
culminated in the
victory of
Kulikovo (1390)

This situation was brought to an end by the so-called 'reassembly
of the Russian lands'. It took place between the middle of the thirteenth and the beginning of the sixteenth century, and was the
work of the Danilovichi, the descendants of Daniel, prince of Moscow
(1263–1303). They were a shrewd, deceitful, cruel and by no means
attractive set of men, but almost all of them were gifted statesmen
who exploited natural advantages, particularly economic, to reassemble the lands which had fallen apart and to shake off Mongol
control. This was achieved more by political manœuvring than by
actual fighting, but the victory of Dmitri Donskoi over the Mongols
in 1390 at Kulikovo on the Don was a turning-point. After Ivan
III's final refusal to pay tribute in 1480 the empire of the Golden
Horde began to disintegrate.

39

30 Russian popular pastimes—a seesaw and monkey-bars—as observed on Adam Olearius's voyage through Muscovy with the Holstein embassy, 1635–36

Moscow was the obvious centre for the newly rising state and around it, from the fourteenth century on, a vast dominion gradually accumulated. Even during the Petersburg period the cardinal importance of the city was not seriously impaired. Although from 1703 to 1917 it was like a queen dethroned, its rôle as the capital of the Soviet Union quickly restored its historical position. What assured Moscow's pre-eminence was its position as a centre of communications on the river Moskva, which connects the upper reaches of the Volga with the middle reaches of the Oka and lies at the intersection of the great trade-routes from west to east and from north to south. From early times, most trade had to pass through Moscow. It is first mentioned in 1147, and the Kremlin was first fortified in 1367. As early as the sixteenth century, Moscow had become the greatest city of Russia. For a long time it was a town of wooden buildings, often derided and called an overgrown village by comparison with the elegance of St Petersburg. But it was, and always remained, the actual centre of Russia. Like London and Paris it has since grown to be one of the great cities of the world, with a population of some five million.

At the beginning of this process of consolidation stands the figure of Ivan Danilovich (1328–40), who had the apt nickname Kalita, i.e. moneybags. It was completed by Ivan III (1462–1505), the most clearly defined and powerful personality amongst the rulers of the first Moscow period, who transformed the random collection of powerless principalities into a united territory totally unlike the Russia of the Kievan period. Ivan III was the first ruler of Great Russia properly speaking. He called himself 'Ruler of all Russia', and by this he understood not only the regions over which he had direct control but also the western territories to which Poland and Lithuania laid claim, and the northern lands as far as the Arctic.

Like his predecessors in Moscow, Ivan III forced his blood-relations, the other princes of the line of Rurik, to become his vassals, members of his court and of the military nobility which surrounded him, and thus turned them into his subordinates. It was he who ended the Mongol yoke in 1480. In 1478 he had conquered old Novgorod, ended its independence and destroyed its republican institutions, transferring its merchants to Moscow and placing Muscovite traders there in their place. In this way he brought the trading activities of Novgorod, which extended to the Arctic and the Urals, within the

31 The Faceted Palace in the Kremlin, commissioned after 1487 by Ivan III from his Lombard architects, Ruffo and Solario. Allusions to early Italian palaces, such as the Diamanti in Ferrara, are more pronounced than in the Kremlin wall, reconstructed after 1485 by the same architects

32 A sketch of Vassily III

growing economic complex of his own expanding realm. He also strove to extend his influence to west and south.

Ivan III was the first ruler to foreshadow the foreign policy of the Tsars of Moscow. Ivan first turned towards the Baltic, towards Livonia and the Prussian Order, but with little result. He then directed his efforts across the steppes and the Ukraine towards the Crimea and the Black Sea coast, once again without real success. In the west he turned against Poland-Lithuania, seeking to regain Smolensk and the disputed Orthodox regions under Polish rule; and here, in 1503, he made some gains. Ivan's first achievement was to strengthen the Russian state against weakness at home and pressure from outside. He also used his increasing power to expand its frontiers, particularly in the north and north-east, towards the Arctic and the Ural mountains. Thus he inaugurated a century of expansion, which extended Russia's boundaries, but which also used up the country's resources and weakened it internally.

33, 34 A contemporary Cracow artist schematized (*above*) the Polish victory at Orsha on the Dnieper, 1514, which stopped the Muscovites' advance after their occupation of the frontier town of Smolensk. *Right*, Alexander I Jagiellon is crowned at Cracow in 1501. The monarchs of a united Poland-Lithuania were to become Moscow's permanent enemies

Ivan's marriage in 1472 with Sophia, the niece of the last emperor of Constantinople, was also motivated by power politics. It was more than a mere formality that Byzantine ceremonial now began to be used in Moscow, and that the two-headed eagle was introduced which remained an emblem of Tsardom down to 1917. Moscow adopted the imperial ideas of Byzantium which had persisted in Constantinople after the city was captured by the Turks in 1453. The concept of the absolute power of the princes, of *autocracy*, which had grown up in Russia in the preceding period, was now supplemented by the adoption of the idea of the *Pantokrator* (the absolute political and religious ruler, combining the functions of Emperor and Pope) supported by and ruling through the Church. This remained a characteristic of the Russian monarchy until 1917.

Ivan's activities brought Russia into closer contact with the rest of Europe. Relations were established with Denmark by way of the Prussian Order, with Lithuania and Poland, with Hungary, with Turkey, with Venice and with the Roman Emperor. In this way, Moscow gradually established herself as a European power. To the rest of Europe it appeared a strange, oriental country; but artistic and civilizing forces of all kinds reached it from the West. These contacts were, however, superficial—a kind of ornamentation, as expressed in architecture—and did not amount to what was later called 'Europeanization'. But they had already begun to exert considerable influence in the field of technology and science.

Ivan III had raised his status as a ruler far above that of his predecessors. His position is comparable with that of his contemporary, Louis XI of France (1461–83), whom he resembled not only in external appearance but also in character and significance. He was an absolute ruler of specifically Muscovite characteristics, but in the European mould, and though he seemed strange and exotic, there was nothing Asiatic about him. His son Vassily III (1505–33) ruled on much the same lines, though he was a less important figure. With him the 'reassembly of the Russian lands' was finally completed. Ivan III had used the title 'Ruler of all Russia', and under his grandson, Ivan IV (1533–84), the title 'Ruler, Tsar and Grand Duke' was introduced, which remained in use down to 1917. The word 'Tsar',

35 A boyar embassy is received at Vienna in 1515 by Maximilian I with Cardinal Lang, during the long negotiations for peace with Poland in which the Imperial court acted as mediator

derived from Caesar, means Emperor and was intended to express the highest form of dominion. A Tsar was far more exalted than a Grand Duke; the title embodied claims against Poland and Lithuania, and by incorporating the ideological notions of Byzantine imperialism it implied rivalry with the Holy Roman Empire and its claims to world dominion.

Ivan IV (1533–84) is known as *grozny*, which does not mean 'the Terrible', but 'the Stern', or awe-inspiring, though Ivan's pathological outbursts of cruelty justify the more usual appellation. He was intelligent, active and well-read and had a remarkable penchant for theological speculation; but he was no great statesman and even less of a hero. Spoilt at an early age, undisciplined and unbalanced, Ivan was inclined to half-crazy outbursts and the wildest excesses of sensuality and cruelty. In this unique figure, often analyzed by poets and historians, the power of the Rurik dynasty finally spent itself.

His reign can be divided into two parts, often called the Good (until about 1564) and the Bad. The first of these was a period of order and reform, the second a period of destructiveness, endless warfare and despotic and cruel administration. Externally he continued the policy of expansion and conquest which he carried beyond the boundaries of Great Russia. He conquered Kazan in 1553, and

Astrakhan in 1556. The whole area around the Volga, from the southern extremity of the Urals to the Caspian Sea, was united with Moscow and opened up for trade, though it had to be secured by the establishment of military colonies in the frontier region of the southeast steppes. Ivan IV's wars with the Crimean Tartars were an important feature of his reign. At the same time he reached out to the sea in the north and fought a long war (1558–83) against the Prussian Order and Poland-Lithuania for control of Livonia. The results were negligible and wasted the strength of his people to no purpose. On the other hand his reign saw the beginning of Russian expansion towards Siberia, which was later to be so significant. It started as a private undertaking by traders and warriors, owing nothing to the government, but their territorial gains were taken over by the latter in 1582.

At the same time relations with western Europe became closer. Embassies arrived and reported on the peculiar characteristics of the 'Muscovites'. The most important of the new connections was that with England after the passage to the White Sea had been discovered.

36 During the reigns of Vassily
III and his son Ivan IV (the
Terrible) Russia gained in both
east and west. Kazan, one of
Ivan's notable victories (1552),
is shown in this ikon being
blessed by angels; some even
find themselves conscripted into
the army

37 Ivan the Terrible
portrayed in
a contemporary ikon

47

38, 39, 40, 41 Trade increased substantially during Ivan the Terrible's reign. *Above right*, a Russian coastal vessel as met by the Dutch Barents expedition in the White Sea, 1597–98. The escutcheon (*above left*) of *c.* 1527 once ornamented the Hanseatic factory at Novgorod. The Seals of the Muscovy Company (1555) and the Eastland Company (1579) (*in margin*) are symbols of England's profitable trade with the Tsars

In 1584, Archangel was founded on its shores. Trade started between England and Russia and with it a political and economic relationship which grew down the centuries, binding the two countries together against Napoleon I's continental blockade, and remaining an important element in the European system until the Crimean War (1854–6).

When we turn from foreign to domestic developments, we find that factors which had begun to appear in the reign of Ivan III became fully effective under his grandson. The expanding central power and the feudal social structure came increasingly into conflict with the interests of the people. Expansion was only possible through the exploitation of the masses, and Russia's position in Europe was won at the expense of endless wars, serfdom and oppression. In Klyuchevsky's words: 'The power of the state grew and the strength of the people declined.' From Ivan III to Nicholas II, Russia never escaped this vicious circle. Under Ivan IV, tension was already appreciable, and discontent and depression were widespread. Thus began the great social crisis which, immediately after his death, constituted the economic background of the 'Time of Troubles' (1584–1613).

Until the end of the sixteenth century, Muscovite Russia was predominantly a country of villages. Forest-clearance and new settlement had increased the agricultural population, and agriculture determined the conditions of life and production. After the fall of Kiev, trade had declined and there had been a regression towards a natural economy in which the great landowners, the princes and the nobility played the main rôle, striving to enrich the land, and the peasants too were increasingly bound to the soil. True, there was money. Prices were calculated in roubles, which had already undergone some depreciation, and taxes had to be paid in currency. There was also a system of credit and money-lending, which proliferated amongst the peasants and made their position increasingly precarious. Some trade was carried on with foreign countries and with foreigners in Russia, Moscow and Archangel being the main centres. But the new commercial capitalism which grew up among the merchants of Moscow was unsophisticated and had little effect on the economy as a whole, which, despite luxury goods from abroad, retained its natural form. It was not until the second half of the sixteenth century that towns and town guilds began to increase their trading activity, but even then in most cases it was the nobles and the Church, rather than the middle class, who provided the driving force, although the merchant class was to assume considerable importance in the 'Time of Troubles' which set in immediately after the reign of Ivan IV.

42 The Oriental splendour of boyar costume is seen in this procession of envoys at the court of Maximilian II in Vienna, 1576

43, 44 Sledges and richly caparisoned hunters are aspects of Russian life drawn early in the sixteenth century

This balance of forces indicates the character of the social structure at the end of the sixteenth century. It was a feudal structure, with tenure by service on the one hand, and peasant serfdom on the other. At the head of society were the princes, now reduced to the status of vassals, and the boyars, descendants of the earlier *druzhina*. They stood nearest to the ruler and advised him in the boyars' Duma which still existed. Then came the gentry, or lesser nobility (*slushiliye lyudi*), who lived on their estates, the court functionaries (*dvoryane*) and the merchants. These were all freemen. Below them were the *censuarii* (*tyagliye lyudi*), peasants born free and still retaining some of their freedom but sinking more and more hopelessly into bondage and dependence; and finally those who had never been free—the slaves of former times (*kholopy*). Outside this hierarchy were the Cossacks, a wild and warlike race which grew up and settled outside the frontiers of the state.

We must now try to outline the complicated process of social development represented by this system, and its effects on ruler and ruled. First of all, the princes already considered their principalities

45, 46 The traditional pattern of popular life, as observed by two Western travellers of the seventeenth century. *Above*, von Mayerbert's sketch of a hamlet on the road to Moscow. *Below*, an itinerant puppeteer, with musicians and a trained bear, as seen by Olearius

not as part of the patrimony of the dynasty, but as their personal inheritance, which they aimed to maintain, increase and pass on to their eldest sons. This attitude was now adopted by the Tsar. He regarded Russia as his land which he conferred, with privileges of every kind, upon his warriors and the gentry in exchange for military service. The knight's fee (*pomestye*), granted in exchange for military service, together with specific privileges—tolls, rents and forced labour from the peasants living on the land—was an enormously important social institution which lasted from medieval times until the emancipation of the peasants in 1861. It was similar to feudalism as it existed elsewhere in Europe, but it developed somewhat later and in a more rigorous form. In Russia, as in the West, it produced a class of land-owning warriors—nobles, who ruled over the labourers —and a manorial economy based on rents and labour services. Those who profited from it, namely the different classes of freemen, gradually developed into a single noble Estate. In the same way the Church acquired a great deal of land in the form of pious endowments, and large numbers of free peasants placed themselves under its protection in hard times.

It was only in 1861 that Alexander II's emancipation of the peasants destroyed this system. The very word 'emancipation' indicates what the growth of feudalism meant for the mass of the rural population. Normally the peasant was no longer required to do military service, although there was conscription before Peter I as well as the communal responsibility of the peasants for taxes. The gentry paid no taxes and the peasant bore the brunt of all impositions. He provided labour and dues for his own land, for the common land or *mir*, and for his lord's estates, according to the latter's needs and wishes. This growth of the peasant's burden, set in train in the thirteenth century, reached a climax in the fifteenth and sixteenth. As the grain trade increased, the demands made by the lord became heavier and heavier. Increasing pressure was brought to bear, always to the disadvantage of the peasant, who was unprotected by the Tsar and entirely under his lord's jurisdiction. All this, and especially the desire to secure his labour permanently, led to the chaining of the peasant to his patch of land. His freedom decreased, until finally the peasantry and the

47, 48 Harvesting and soldiering, miniatures from sixteenth-century saints' lives

old slave class were fused. The development of serfdom was nearly complete by the end of the sixteenth century, though it was intensified in the reigns of Peter the Great and Catherine II.

The mass of the peasants tried to escape this oppression by migration to the free territories of the newly won south-east, by revolts and by ceaseless unrest, to counter which the princes and the feudal nobility, the bureaucracy and the army always co-operated closely. This agrarian crisis became a social cancer which ravaged Russia in both the Muscovite and the Petersburg eras. Originating at the end of the Middle Ages, it lasted until the First World War. While not, of course, confined to Russia, it was intensified there by the interminable demands of government and by the brutality and arbitrariness of the lords, though the latter was occasionally tempered by paternalist traditions. By the end of Ivan IV's reign, feudalism and serfdom were the essential characteristics of the social structure, by comparison with which the activity of the merchants and artisans was of minor significance.

53

Above this feudal society towered the authority of the Grand Duke and Tsar, the absolutism based on Moscow which reached its culmination in Ivan IV. We have already briefly mentioned its origins. So far as Russia was concerned, it was something unique, and yet it was little different in kind from the absolutism of western Europe between the fifteenth and eighteenth centuries. It implied a system of duties extending through all classes of society from top to bottom, and a strict limitation of personal rights and freedom. This social structure persisted until the eighteenth century for the nobility and until the middle of the nineteenth for the other classes.

Let us now return to the figure of Ivan IV. Sometimes intelligent, sometimes incoherent, he was a hard and cruel man who ignored the limits imposed by human and divine law and, inspired by ideas of divine right, envisaged a duty-bound society far beneath him, a society that possessed no rights. He sought to base the political order on the duties of each individual class; it could even be said that he wished to establish an enlightened absolutism, raised above and holding the balance between the classes. For this, however, he would have needed a different personality. As it was, his unbalanced, moody, inconsistent nature provoked violent reactions, and these reactions drove him to counter-attack. In 1564 the second period of Ivan IV's reign began, a time of terror which lasted for twenty years.

His methods were extraordinary. He tore apart the country which he and his predecessors had striven so hard to reunite. Some parts he handed over to the boyars whom he regarded as traitors, others, comprising the *oprichnina*, he reserved for himself and his warriors. In a veritable reign of terror he destroyed the aristocratic class. He dispossessed them of their lands, driving out and killing those who opposed him. He treated Russia as if it were a conquered territory. In principle it was a struggle of the absolute monarchy against the Estates, against the boyars whom he decimated; but it was a barren, half-crazy régime which lasted for two decades, seriously weakened the economic system and oppressed the masses without reason. Ivan's numerous wars during this phase left the country no peace; a famous Russian historian has rightly compared it with the Mongol rule. But without a grasp of what happened between 1564

49 Bird's-eye-view of Moscow in a map of 1570. The Kremlin is in the centre, the foreign merchants' quarter (*nemetskaya sloboda*) at bottom left

and 1584 it would be impossible to understand the 'Time of Troubles' which followed.

Nevertheless, the two decades of Ivan's terror proved that, however much autocracy had developed in Moscow since Ivan Kalita and Ivan III, opposing forces still existed. They were reflected indirectly in the peasant movements of which we have spoken; they found more direct expression in the opposition of the nobility and in the National Assemblies (*Zemskiye Sobory*), which historians have often underestimated. Though the Russian assemblies may never have attained the same importance, diets and assemblies comparable to the Estates of western Europe met in Moscow in the sixteenth and seventeenth centuries. They were usually made up of the nobility,

55

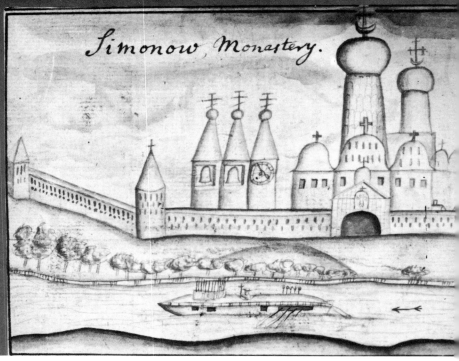

Simonow, Monastery.

50 A monastery in Little Russia as sketched in 1683

though from time to time they included other Estates as well. In spite of their antagonism, however, the Tsar and the nobility usually co-operated against the peasants: Russia under Ivan IV was a country dominated by these two elements. As the administration grew, officials became more prevalent, and they too were aligned with the higher strata of society as an instrument of oppression. The merchant class, since it was partly involved in the economic and trading interests of the crown, maintained rather more independence, though it suffered as well.

The Tsar, who was himself interested in theological speculation, did not interfere with or oppress the Church. On the contrary, its power increased considerably during this period, as its economic position showed. It possessed vast territories, numerous vassals and dependants, and had its own system of justice. The Church's position became even stronger after the conquest of Constantinople by the

51 Feast of the Trinity at St Basil's, Moscow

Turks, for the Metropolitan of Moscow now took the place of the Patriarch, claiming the rank of protector of all Orthodox Christians. From 1589 onwards he was autonomous, with the title of Patriarch. Behind him stood the Russian state. His relationship with the government was never formally and constitutionally defined, but it was implicit in the doctrine that Moscow was the 'third Rome'. This doctrine gathered strength after the beginning of the sixteenth century. 'Two Romes have passed', it was proclaimed, 'the third [i.e. Moscow] stands fast; and there shall be no fourth.' Moscow's claim to be the successor of Byzantium, though never recognized outside Russia, heightened the Church's standing at home, and was frequently exploited in Russia's Balkan policy from the seventeenth to the twentieth centuries.

In conformity with Byzantine tradition the Church submitted itself utterly to the ruler of the state, who was the anointed of God.

57

He did not concern himself with purely religious questions, but the Church was totally dependent on him. With its tendency to centralization, it supported the absolute power of the state. In exchange, as a result of vast donations and privileges, it gained enormous economic and social power, and its alliance with the Tsardom assured its legal position. A struggle of the spiritual and temporal powers, similar to the war between the 'two swords' which so weakened the Holy Roman Empire in the Middle Ages, was unknown in Russia until the seventeenth century.

There is no doubt that the Church at this time was useful to the Russian state. It is also true that the connexion between Church and state affected the Church's own inner life, leading to rigidity and spiritual decline. It is, however, easy to exaggerate these consequences. Ever since the days of Vladimir I, Christianity had penetrated deep into the hearts of the Russian people. Orthodoxy lacked neither substance nor depth of religious feeling. The Orthodox Church was a mystical community, regulated by its liturgy, with powers of salvation. It was a distinct form of Christian organization, separate from and opposed to the Roman Catholic Church of the West, and it rejected the Pope's claim to overlordship. It is not easy to make a final judgment on the significance of the Church in the first Moscow period, but we can say that, by the end of the sixteenth century, it was much more a conservative disciplinary institution, co-operating with the prince and the ruling classes, than a consoler of troubled hearts.

Because of its own peculiar ecclesiastical development, Russia had no part in the process of ferment which affected the West from the period of the crusades to the great voyages of discovery, or in the Renaissance and the Reformation, and which led to the emergence of individualism and a new emphasis on human personality. The medieval Russian was European in spirit, without doubt, but he was influenced by collective bonds, which were accentuated by pressure from the state and from the ruling classes, and by adversity. As yet he had developed no literature or learning worth talking about, though he had achievements to his credit in the sphere of ecclesiastical architecture. He was very far removed from western

Europe. Nor did Europe penetrate far into Russia before the end of the sixteenth century, apart from the few influences already mentioned. None the less, though remote from Europe, Russia was its outer bulwark. As Klyuchevsky has written, fate placed the Russian people 'at the eastern gate of Europe, which it defended against the attacks of the nomad plunderers of Asia'. They 'saved European civilization from the onslaughts of the Tartars'. But in the process they 'fell behind the rest of Europe'.

'Sentinel duty', Klyuchevsky concludes, 'is always a thankless job and is soon taken for granted, especially if it is well performed: the more alert the guards, the more peacefully sleep those they protect, and the less inclined the latter are to realize the true value of the sacrifice their peaceful rest demands. This was Moscow's position in Europe at the end of the sixteenth century.'

THE 'TIME OF TROUBLES' (1584–1613)
AND THE FIRST TSARS OF THE ROMANOV DYNASTY (1613–89)

The reign of Ivan IV marked the climax of the first Moscow period. After this peak had been reached, a sharp decline set in; indeed, even at the time of Ivan IV's rise to power it is evident that the seeds of dissolution were germinating. Shortly after his death revolutionary upheavals broke out in many quarters; the ferment was accentuated by the weakness of his successor, Fyodor I, much as the Revolution of 1789 was caused by that of Louis XVI. The result was the upheavals of the 'Time of Troubles', the first great revolution in Russian history.

Fyodor I (1584–98), Ivan's son, was a weakling and bigot, with whom the Rurik dynasty finally perished. The Tsar's half-brother, Dmitri, the last descendant of the house of Ivan Kalita, was assassinated in 1591, and public opinion put the blame on Boris Godunov, Fyodor's brother-in-law. A man of Tartar provenance, Boris took over the government, endeavouring in an intelligent and statesman-like way to safeguard the interests of the state and of the ruling feudal class. He contributed considerably to the extension of serfdom, to the chaining of the peasants to the soil and their submission to the arbitrary will of the landowners. But he was not able to hold

MARIA MNISZCHOWNA
GEORGII DE MAGNA KONCZICE MNISZ
ALCH PALATINI SENDOMIRIENSIS FILIA
VXOR VERO DEMETRII IMPERATORIS
MOSCHOVIA CORONAT/R IN IMPERATRICE
MOSCHOVIA PER ARCHIEPISCOP/M RIT/S
GRECI IN VRBE MOSKVA METROPOLI IM
PERII MOSCHOVITICI IN PRESENTIA LEGATI
REGIS POLONIA NICOLAI OLESNIKI
ANNO DOMINI 1605

52, 53 The coronation in Moscow (*above*)
of the false Dmitri
and Maria Mniszchowna,
daughter of a rich Polish landowner,
in 1605.
Above right, Dmitri painted by
a contemporary Polish artist

54 Boris Godunov,
regent 1584–98 and Tsar until 1605.
Heir to the dilemma of the succession
after Ivan IV,
Godunov managed by his election
60   to put off the threat of civil war

his ground against the nobility, who opposed him as an upstart and saw in the reaction against absolutism the possibility of a victory for their own aristocratic class. Nevertheless, after the death of Fyodor, Boris was proclaimed Tsar by a general assembly.

The leaders of the noble Estates came from the upper ranks of the boyars, for the most part descendants of the various branches of the house of Rurik. They led the opposition to Boris Godunov and placed restrictions on him. In addition, he was hampered by the appearance of a false Dmitri who claimed to have escaped the attempted assassination. This character, the hero of drama by Schiller, Hebbel, Pushkin and others, was certainly a pretender, though he himself perhaps believed in his authenticity. But although no more than an adventurer, he had contacts with the Polish monarchy and nobility, with the Catholic Church and the Jesuits. More important, the mass of the peasants within Russia saw in him their saviour and deliverer. They sided with him, especially in the south and south-east, and the Cossacks, the warlike settlers of the border country, also supported him. It was a great agrarian and social revolt against the power of the monarchy and against the boyars, with the false Dmitri as its figure-head. He pressed on to Moscow and after Boris Godunov's sudden death in 1605 was even elected Tsar, but he was incapable of establishing order or of ruling. His contacts with Poland and with Catholicism soon put an end to his popularity—a fact which the boyars exploited. When he was assassinated, Vassily Sjuisky (1606–16), a representative of the high nobility, was proclaimed Tsar in his place by popular acclaim.

The result was to increase the class struggles and internal confusion. A new false Dmitri appeared, likewise supported by the south and south-east. A foreign country, Sweden, was brought into the civil war. Poland also intervened and advanced eastwards without interference, driven by the urge to expansion which at this time obsessed the Polish monarchy and feudal nobility. The Polish king forced his way into Moscow and the boyars elected Vladislav, the heir to the Polish throne, as Tsar, though at the same time imposing certain conditions on him. The result was foreign rule, by means of which the boyars hoped to set up a government of the Estates in place of the absolutism instituted by Ivan IV.

55 The deposed Tsar Vassily Shuisky is brought before Sigismund III at the Sejm or parliament in Warsaw, 1611

56 Mikhail I, first of the Romanov dynasty, was crowned as a boy of sixteen. His authoritarian father, the Patriarch Philaret, one of the original pretenders of 1584, acted as joint ruler until his death in 1633

A national revolt soon followed. It was initiated by the Patriarch and organized and led by two men—a monument to whom still stands on the Red Square in front of the Kremlin—the merchant Kusma Minin and Prince Dmitri Pozharsky. They propagated the idea of *opolcheniye*, the arming of the people or the general levy. In fact, a people's force raised in this way relieved the city of Moscow and drove out the Poles, and a National Assembly containing members of all the Estates elected a new Tsar on 21 February 1613. Rejecting a foreign candidate, it chose a great-nephew of Ivan IV, the seventeen-year-old Mikhail Fyodorovitch, with whom the Romanov dynasty began.

The details of the election are still a matter of dispute. In particular, it is not clear whether Mikhail bound himself to the boyars by an electoral capitulation. But its general significance is evident. The election was carried out at the instance of the lower nobility, the townspeople and the Cossacks. But if these classes were content with Mikhail's election, it by no means expressed the wishes of the peasants. The new dynasty, in other words, was involved with the class struggles of the day. The new monarch ruled as an elected Tsar working with the assembly, not as the hereditary ruler of his country. This was the historical and political significance of the 'Time of Troubles'. Absolutism was not restored immediately. Grigory Kotoshikhin, a well-informed statesman of the next generation, said of Mikhail: 'He may have been called an absolute ruler, but without the support of the boyars he would not have been able to do anything.' In fact, Tsar Mikhail always ruled in conjunction with the *Zemski Sobor*, and so to a certain extent did his son Alexis.

Until Peter I took the reins into his own hands, the new Muscovite state, which took shape during the 'Time of Troubles', must be considered as a joint government of Tsar and boyars. This was a transitional stage to which historians have rarely paid sufficient attention. The *Zemski Sobor*, though less firmly anchored and less influential than the Estates in the German principalities at the same period, was a representative body which occasionally made laws. Nevertheless the absolutism created by Ivan III and his successors, although considerably weakened, stood out firmly against the Estates, and the assembly was never a powerful political factor. The victory of the boyars at the end of the 'Time of Troubles' was, in fact, more apparent than real. The boyar class, the ancient nobility of birth, was by this time in a state of inner decay. Its decline, which Ivan IV had hastened, could no longer be postponed. In its place, the leading rôle was taken over by the more recently formed *noblesse de robe*, the so-called *dvoryanstvo*. It was they who profited from the intensification of serfdom, and the progress made in this direction, together with their growing political influence, satisfied their claims for the moment. The interests of the lesser nobility, and their contacts with the merchants of the cities, were by now a more important factor than those of the boyars, though the lesser nobility too was already being affected by changes leading towards capitalism.

Another way in which Russia between 1613 and 1689 differed from the earlier absolutism of Muscovy, and from the later absolutism of Peter the Great, was in its relationship with western Europe. In principle, Russia's attitude to Europe had hardly changed since the death of Ivan IV. Yet indications of a change had been perceptible as early as the time of Boris Godunov. Boris had supported Westernization, and from his time onwards Western influences extended far beyond ornaments, luxury goods and the like. In the reigns of the first two Romanovs a real desire to master Western languages and absorb European culture was evident. European influence now affected military organization—arms and the creation of an armaments industry, for example—the factory system, transport, and indeed the whole economy. If previously only a few artists and builders from abroad had come to Russia, now large numbers of western Europeans settled in Moscow. For the most part they were Germans who acted as instructors in commerce and industry. They settled in the German suburb (*nemetskaya sloboda*) which played so important a part in Peter I's youth. Westernization became far more comprehensive and profound under the first two Romanovs. In this respect as in others, Peter was not an originator but a ruler who carried existing trends to completion.

Even a brief survey of the development of seventeenth-century Russia is sufficient to show that, in spite of social disruption and the increased importance of the Estates, the absolutism of the ruler was not significantly weakened. The position was much the same as in the revolution of 1605. Royal authority was more powerful than the countervailing forces and was still capable of pursuing strong and purposeful policies at home and abroad. But it had changed in character since the time of Ivan IV. The monarchy now recognized that the earlier forms of absolutism and the means at its disposal were inadequate for the conduct of large-scale policies, which demanded something in the nature of a transformation of the state along Western lines. In this respect it already foreshadowed Peter I's policy. Thus the differences between fifteenth- and sixteenth-century Moscow and the Moscow of the first Romanovs were considerable.

Mikhail Fyodorovitch Romanov (1613–45) ruled with the counsel of the boyars and the national assembly. Down to 1633, however, his father, Philaret, a more gifted and energetic man, who was then Patriarch and supreme head of the Orthodox Church in Russia, shared the government with him in a kind of joint rule. We may consider him as the first important, or at least the first clearly delineated figure amongst Russian ecclesiastical princes. For the first two decades of Mikhail's reign, Philaret was the real ruler; he was a

57 The Moscow Kremlin on Palm Sunday, 1636. Mikhail Romanov leads a procession from the Saviour's Tower. St Basil's is at the left

skilled diplomat and had the confidence of the land-owning classes. He was concerned to reform the administration, which had gone to pieces, though neither in this nor in restoring the finances did he have much success. In pursuing these aims, however, he laid great stress on foreign trade, particularly with England, and on attracting foreign officers, technicians and industrialists to organize and arm the military forces. The new armaments industry introduced from abroad helped to revive domestic industries such as metallurgy. Some idea of the size of the foreign influx into Russia is indicated by the fact that the German suburb in Moscow at that time housed as many as 1,000 Protestant families.

If Mikhail's reign achieved nothing conclusive, things improved under his successor, Alexis Mikhailovich (1645–76). It is true that the new Tsar was a weak and passive man, one half of whose mind was rooted in the past, even if the other half was bent on necessary innovations. Though in many respects a typical representative of the old Russia, he was also a precursor of Peter the Great. To begin with, he had to face the pressure of the Estates and of noble factions, but

66

later he avoided summoning the *Zemski Sobor*. His projects of reform centred on the preparation of a new Code of Law. But the new Code was drawn up on the advice of the Estates, and when it appeared in 1649 its provisions favoured the lesser nobility and the towns, and bore heavily on the peasants. In fact, no real improvement followed from the new Code. This was apparent in the continuing discontent and economic difficulties. Finances perhaps improved to a certain extent as a result of increasing trade, in which both the Tsar and his court took an active part; but taxation weighed heavily on the peasants who were burdened with debts. In 1678 there were 833,000 farms from which tax was due. Of these 92,000 (11.3 per cent) belonged to the towns, 118,000 (14.2 per cent) to the Church, the clergy and the monasteries, 83,000 (9.9 per cent) to the Tsar's court, 88,000 (10.5 per cent) to the boyars, and no less than 452,000 (54.1 per cent) to the lesser nobility. The wretched conditions and growing discontent of the peasants exploded in 1668–71, after years of unrest, in the famous rising of Stenka Razin, among the peasants and Cossacks on the lower Volga and the Don.

58, 59 In the reign of 'the most pacific' and inefficient Tsar Alexis (*below left*) peasant revolts swelled into full-scale civil war. The most savage of the insurrections was led by the Cossack Stenka Razin, seen (*below right*) on one of his pillaging expeditions on the Lower Volga

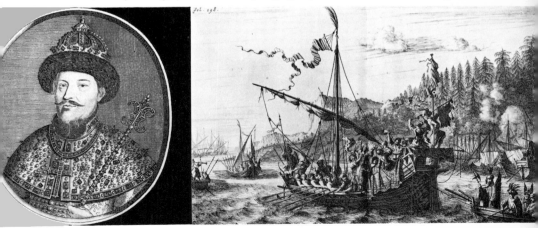

The social crisis under Tsar Alexis was accompanied by a religious and ecclesiastical crisis which also had important consequences. Just as the patriarch Philaret had stood by Michael's side, sharing in the government, so in the time of Alexis the office of Patriarch was in the hands of another important ecclesiastical prince, Nikon. For a time Nikon's position was almost that of regent. The result was a breach with the Tsar; Nikon was stripped of his office and banished. Nevertheless a real conflict of Church and state was implicit in his attitude. 'The priesthood', Nikon maintained, 'is higher than the Tsardom. Unction comes from God, but it comes to the Tsar through the clergy.' But Nikon was unable to make his point of view prevail. He found no support amongst the clergy, which ecclesiastical tradition had not prepared for such claims to power over the state. The Tsar proved stronger than the Church.

Nikon also caused a schism in Russian Orthodoxy which lasted for centuries. From 1654 onwards he set about improving the liturgical books, whose text was extremely corrupt, but in the process he aroused the conservative opposition of clergy and people. Though it is difficult to understand this disagreement today, since it was concerned not with dogma but with words and forms, it led to a split in Russian Orthodoxy which has never been completely healed. Millions of orthodox Christians became schismatics—not sectaries, but orthodox believers who held fast to certain external forms and for this reason were known as 'old believers' (*starovyery*). Though good, sober citizens, from that time onward they were persecuted and only the edict of toleration of 30 April 1905 gave them a certain degree of peace and civil recognition. This schism may be described as a conflict between the people's Church and the official Church, a reaction against the transformation of the Orthodox Church into an instrument of state.

The schism was yet another sign of how profoundly Russia had been stirred by the 'Time of Troubles'. It was in a state of social, political and spiritual turmoil, and deeply influenced by Europe. This was evident not only in technology and industry but also in literature. An outstanding figure was the Minister of Foreign Affairs, A. L. Ordyn Nashchokin (dismissed in 1671, died in 1680), a first-

60, 61 The reforming Patriarch Nikon and his clergy, painted *c.* 1660. *Right*, the Slavonic Bible of 1663, a product of the new scholarship

class diplomat and the first Chancellor of Russia, who was in favour of adopting Western models. Thus he was one of the first of those who, in the nineteenth century, were to be known as 'Westernizers'. The very existence of a 'Westernizing' movement indicates that a new period in the history of Russia was beginning. The common idea that Peter the Great turned Russia towards the West without previous preparation, that he imposed Westernization upon a barbaric un-European people, is entirely false. Already in the preceding decades Russia had been awakened. The needs of the army, of finance and of the economy had already led to reforms, and from there it was only a step to the reform of schools and education. Hence it is wrong to regard Peter the Great as a revolutionary innovator. He found something like a programme of reform, and a propitious atmosphere, already in existence. It is true that he carried out his reforms with revolutionary energy. But much of what Peter I later put into practice had been prepared by the policies of his predecessors.

A prerequisite for the revival of Russia was an energetic foreign policy. The Poles and Swedes who had laid hold on great stretches of the county had to be expelled. Under Mikhail the peace of Stolbovo was signed with Sweden in 1617. Novgorod was restored to Russia, but there was still no outlet on the Baltic coast. In 1618 an armistice was negotiated with Poland. This left Smolensk and Russian territory as far as Vyazma and Chernigov in Polish hands. But the Poles and Swedes withdrew from the territories immediately subject to Moscow, the frontiers of which were now the same as they had been in the fifteenth century. In the West, the Thirty Years War involved Russia indirectly and drew it further into the web of European conflicts, though it was not interested in the religious aspects of the struggle. Sweden and France sought a treaty with Russia against Austria. It was not concluded, for Moscow's main interests still lay elsewhere, against the Tartars in the Crimea and the Turks rather than against Poland in the West. Azov on the mouth of the Don, at the entry to the sea of Azov and hence to the Black Sea, was the objective, but it remained in Turkish hands.

Thus, Moscow's initial successes were not great, but it was no longer a shuttlecock in the hands of foreign powers. It regained its freedom of action, strengthened by the arming and organization of its army on a Western model, and guided by its own diplomacy. It was again in a position to go on the offensive, and gradually it made certain gains. By the Peace of Andrussovo in 1667 it won back Smolensk and Kiev from Poland. Wars with Sweden and Turkey brought no result; but it achieved further successes against Poland, gaining possession of the eastern Ukraine, on the left bank of the Dnieper, though the right bank still remained in Polish hands. The union of the Ukrainian territories with Moscow was sealed by the treaty of Pereyaslavl (1654) between Bogdan Khmelnitsky, the Hetman of the Cossacks, and Tsar Alexis.

It is important to consider the nature and form of this union, for it played a considerable part in the Ukrainian movement of the twentieth century. It was not a union between two independent states. What we call the Ukraine was never a real state, but rather an unstable Cossack republic, constantly fighting and wavering between

Moscow, Poland-Lithuania and Turkey, which lacked a real basis of political consciousness and capacity for political organization. Politically, both Moscow and Poland were far more stable. In fact, the wild romanticism of the steppes, which Gogol has portrayed so well, was no foundation for a stable state. The memory of the Ukrainian national hero, the Hetman Bogdan Khmelnitsky, is quite rightly cherished; but if we consider how hard pressed he was politically, it will at once be obvious that there could have been no question of an agreement between two equal states. Khmelnitsky secured far-reaching autonomy for the Ukraine, which was invariably confirmed in later treaties; but he became a vassal of Moscow, his protector, and from this time onward, Moscow controlled the foreign relations of the Ukraine and exacted tribute from it, in exchange for which it protected the Ukrainians against enemies from without.

The Peace of Andrussovo confirmed this acquisition in the Ukraine, also its division. Poland retained the Ukrainian lands on the right bank of the Dnieper, although without doubt they were neither Polish nor Catholic. This was a breeding-ground for further conflicts. The peace treaty, however, secured Moscow a considerable extension of its territories and the recovery of a large part of the old Russian fatherland. It reunited different branches of the Russian people, whose political destinies had gone different ways. It also strengthened the movement for Westernization, since the cultivated classes in Kiev were more numerous and more Westernized than in Moscow. The Ukrainians did continue to strive for independence under their Hetmans; but the foundations for independent political development were lacking, and finally at the end of the eighteenth century the autonomy of the Ukraine was suppressed.

Tsar Alexis had two wives, from different boyar families, around whom rival noble factions struggled for power. The rise and fall of these factions now became an important factor in the political situation. On Alexis's death he was succeeded by a son from his first marriage, Fyodor III (1676–82), an insignificant character whose reign is mainly noteworthy for the discarding in 1682 of the age-old aristocratic hierarchy—the so-called *mestnichestvo*—by which

62 Khmelnitsky was recognized
as Hetman or generalissimo,
after leading his Cossacks
to victory over the Poles in 1645

63 The Volga, a high road of Romanov expansion
and new trade, whose whole cou
from Muscovy to the Caspian
is picturesquely illustra
in this map of 1662 (oppos

every nobleman was bound to his position or rank. The abandon-
ment of this rigid and senseless system made room for a new and
more modern hierarchy, and can be attributed with a good deal of
certainty to the spread of Western influence. Fyodor himself died
in 1682, only six years after his father, without direct heirs. He had,
however, two brothers: Ivan, a second son from Alexis's first marriage,
a mental and physical weakling, and Peter, the son of a second marriage, born in 1672, still only ten years old but mentally and physically
well endowed. Around them the struggle centred, for although on
Fyodor's death Peter was proclaimed Tsar, his powerful and ambitious half-sister, Sophia, had her brother Ivan made co-Tsar while
she herself assumed the position of regent. It was around her that
the noble faction rallied.

Raised to power by a bloody *coup d'état* in 1682, Sophia attempted
to continue the policy, both internal and external, of her father with
the support of Prince Galitzine, a pronounced Westernizer. But her
position was by no means strong and in 1689 she was easily deposed.
Government was now in the hands of Peter and Ivan, but the latter
was totally incompetent and died in 1696. In fact, Peter had been the
effective ruler since 1689, although at first he gave little attention to
government. Rather, in his early years, he followed his own inclina-
tions and had his own associates; it is only with his journey abroad in
1697 that the turning-point comes. Even so, the beginning of his
reign in 1689 marks the opening of a new period in Russian history.

If the 'Time of Troubles' had been a revolutionary period, the

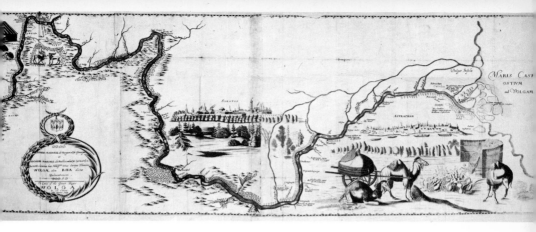

reigns of the first Romanovs constituted a calmer period of transition. They saw some degree of consolidation and a number of successes, at home and abroad, although they were by no means firmly established. While retaining its own character, Russia became more open to Western influences and its relationship with Europe changed substantially. As the seventeenth century progressed, Russia was involved in the European political system in a manner previously unknown. Internally also, it underwent change on a Western pattern. It established closer contact with the states of central Europe (e.g. with the Great Elector) and of the West. This Europeanization was not a mere incident; it was an integral element in Russian history, providing an important precedent for the more far-reaching process of Westernization under Peter the Great and Catherine II.

In the course of these developments three great problems had arisen, which were not to be solved during the seventeenth century. They were the Baltic question, the question of the Black Sea and the Polish question. What was at issue was territorial expansion to the west, involving the whole region from the southern frontiers of Livonia and Courland to the Black Sea, which Russia in 1689 had not yet reached at any point. Even so, great expansion had taken place. By 1689 the frontiers of Russia extended from Pskov through Smolensk and Kiev as far as Azov, from Manych and Terek to the Caspian Sea, from the northern shores of the Caspian to the Urals and northwards following the range of the Urals to the Arctic ocean. It was already a mighty realm when Peter the Great took over.

64 Russia in Europe, 1689–1796

III THE PETERSBURG PERIOD 1689–1917

There are good reasons for describing the years between 1689 and 1917 as the Petersburg period. It is not only that the new capital was founded at the beginning of this period (in 1703) and lost its central position at the end. More important, the intervening decades were characterized by the predominance of a form of Tsarist absolutism which St Petersburg reflected. Moscow, the centre of Russia today, differs in every respect from the aristocratic city which Peter the Great conjured up out of the mud. Dostoyevsky called Petersburg 'the most calculated of all capital cities'.

Right from the beginning there was opposition, which was never quite silenced, against this artificial town with its impressive layout on the majestic Neva, with the fortress of St Peter and St Paul, the Nevsky Prospekt, the Winter Palace and countless other palaces. It was utterly European in style and totally different from Moscow. Opinions on its significance for Russia have also vacillated right into the twentieth century. Only today has the view come to prevail that Peter's action was, on the whole, necessary for Russia and that the foundation of Petersburg was a lasting service. Earlier, the Westernizers praised him to the skies, while the Slavophiles denounced him and his works as a departure from the true spirit of Russia. Already in 1700 he was branded as the 'Antichrist'. The so-called old Russian, Muscovite party hated Peter's city, the foreign bureaucracy which had its headquarters there (especially the many Germans who were thrown back on themselves and knew nothing of the country and the people outside), and the court nobility and the Guards. Dostoyevsky always opposed Petersburg, and the different revolutionary movements were hostile to it, for it represented the centre of Tsarism and the instruments of reaction. Even when Petersburg became the seat of industry and finance, the position did not change, since the capitalists were for the most part

65 A street of palatial façades along the Neva in St Petersburg in the mid-eighteenth century

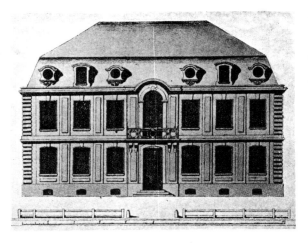

66, 67 The Tsar edited and approved Domenico Tressini's designs for dwellings of noble and humble subjects in the new capital, here shown in engravings of 1714

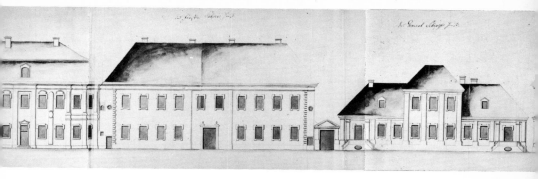

closely associated with Tsarism and the land-owning classes. The masses, the workers, were always hostile to the new city.

There are good reasons for regarding the Petersburg period as a single continuous epoch. It is true that the continuity was broken after 1855 by the reform of Alexander II, but the interlude was short, and after 1881 Russia fell back into its old ways, into absolutism and reaction, so that it is reasonable to maintain that the old order continued from 1881 to 1905 and to a certain extent even beyond, until it collapsed in 1917 with the great Revolution.

PETER THE GREAT (1689–1725)
AND HIS IMMEDIATE SUCCESSORS (1725–62)

The personality with whom the Petersburg period began and who gave it its particular stamp was Peter I (1689–1725). There was nothing of the traditional Russian or Muscovite about him—so little, that popular opinion long believed that he was not his mother's child but a changeling from the German suburb of Moscow. He was of immense physique, though his powerful constitution never over-came the nervous troubles of his youth. His genius, his will-power and his appetites were vast. He was always active, and his natural disposition, developed by experience and education, was directed to the rational and practical, without the slightest mystical leaning.

From his earliest youth he was interested in applied science, in warfare and above all—a rare characteristic for a Russian of that time—in the sea, in shipbuilding, the navy and overseas trade. For this reason he consorted almost exclusively with foreigners in Moscow. To pursue his studies further, he visited the West in 1697 and 1698. For Peter, Western techniques and the economic institutions of the West were indispensable models for transforming Russia, which he was ready to do if necessary by brute force; in this respect he differed fundamentally from his predecessors, for whom Western models were never more than incidental. He wanted 'to open a window onto Europe', and he did so with such energy that it could never again be closed. Whence he got this urge is a secret of his personality which the historian cannot penetrate.

Peter the Great's achievements raise the whole question of the rôle of personality in history. Was it he who created the new régime, or did the régime create him? What was the relationship between the man and his circumstances? Did he really change the direction of Russian history and the character of the Russian people? What is certain is that his excessive demands, and especially the wars which occupied twenty-one of the thirty-six years of his reign, were harmful at the time. Plekhanov, who gave much thought to the rôle of the statesman-hero in history, said that 'he reflected new social relationships which had been generated by previous developments . . . His activity was the conscious and free expression of this necessary and unconscious process.' It was a process which had begun much earlier and which Russia had to conform to if it were not to sink back into semi-Asiatic barbarism. From this it follows that Peter was not, as Carlyle maintained, a complete innovator. Rather, he continued along a path that had already been trodden. But Westernization, with him, was systematic, not superficial, and so he influenced the character of the Russian people in a constructive way. His actions brought him into conflict with many people, but even so he was the first ruler whose deeds had such enormous effects.

The study of Peter the Great's character and influence illustrates the failure of even the most detailed research to penetrate the mystery of human personality. Much about him, no doubt, can be

68 Peter the Great, by Aert de Gelder ▶

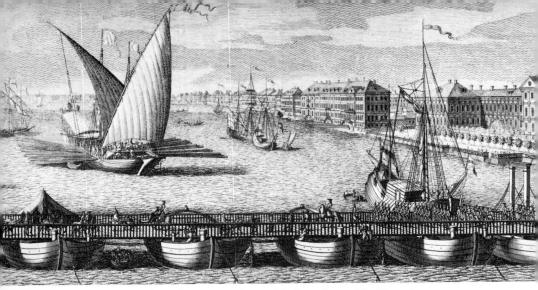

69, 70 Eighteenth-century views of St Petersburg. The Neva in 1753, upstream from a bridge of boats at the Admiralty. The old Winter Palace is the building

explained in terms of environment. Still more, however, remains inexplicable and mysterious. No one today would endorse Kavelin's judgment that 'from head to toe' Peter was 'a Great Russian personality, a Great Russian soul'. In many respects he was the direct opposite of what is usually understood by a 'great Russian'. Though he intuitively grasped their natural propensities, he seemed foreign to his own people, and this very fact confounds Kavelin's view; in any case the Russian assessment of him never ceased to fluctuate and was contradictory in the extreme.

Were the revolutionary changes he carried through a blessing for his people or not? Were they a necessity or only an example of despotic wilfulness? A whole book could be written about the various Russian assessments of Peter the Great. It would reflect all the doubts and controversies which have arisen about Russia's place in history. In fact, three choices alone faced Petrine Russia. It could fall back into decay like Turkey or China, and of this there were many portents when Peter came to the throne. It could fall a prey to conquest by Sweden and Poland, or even by Hungary or Austria, and to German eastward expansion, and thus become a colony of western Europe. Or it could keep abreast of Europe, catch up with Europe, gain

nearest to the bridge. A shallop carries sailors to their galley. *Right*, the Admiralty (tower of 1717) and its new shipyards, seen from the Neva at the end of Peter's reign

from contact with Europe by land and sea, take over its methods and standards in politics, economics, technology and culture. Peter the Great was deeply aware of this fateful choice, in a way none before him had been—in a way the nineteenth-century 'Westernizers' also were and to which they gave formal expression. To this end, however inconsistent he may have been in other ways, Peter acted with rigorous logic and incomparable determination. Only Catherine II to a certain degree, Lenin and Stalin approached him in this respect.

Contemporary Europe provided Peter with models of absolutism and mercantilism. He knew something of the theory of both; he had contacts with Puffendorf, for example, which seem to have been more important than those with Leibnitz. In practice the example which influenced him most, in spite of the importance of Holland, was Prussia. It is not difficult to detect Prussian models and Prussian parallels in his administrative and military institutions. Just as absolutism and mercantilism brought about the consolidation of the Prussian state, particularly on the economic side, so also they brought about the consolidation of the Russian state. And just as in Prussia nothing was done with or through the people, so also in Russia the rôle of the people was entirely passive.

81

71, 72 Two substantial new products of Peter's reign—the ABC of Istomin and (*right*) the new children's books produced for the first time in Russia from 1711

The essential motive behind Peter's transformation of Russia was that of expansion, towards the sea and towards the West. This explains not only his expansive foreign policy but also his specific measures of internal reform. It explains also the logic in his programme of Europeanization and the order in which he carried it out. First came the army, the means to the achievement of all his major objectives; then, in logical sequence, as measures to underpin the military reforms, there followed financial and administrative reform, the enforcement of compulsory state service for all classes from the nobility downwards, and measures concerned with class relationships, economic policy, and finally education and culture.

Peter's successes in foreign policy inspired national pride and created the first, extremely uneven glimmerings of national consciousness. The new attitudes of government served also as a stimulus among a small section of the ruling class for whom Peter's reforms seemed at least to foreshadow greater scope for individual initiative.

Even so, the changes introduced by Peter did not exercise a really formative influence on the intellectual attitudes of the ruling classes as a whole. Such an influence began with Elizabeth Petrovna and became more widely felt only under Catherine II. In Peter's own time the effect of his reforms, with their emphasis on compulsory state service, was rather to reinforce collective responsibility and the sense of subservience to the state. This primarily affected the peasant masses, for it was they who bore almost the whole burden of the progress Russia made under Peter. In theory unlimited, Peter's absolutism was in practice dependent on the support of the land-owners and he had to tolerate their exploitation of the peasantry.

This explains the popular hostility and opposition to Peter's system. Peasant unrest was a persistent feature of his reign. Its significance should not be underestimated. It found expression in the attitude of the groups later known as 'old Russian' or 'Muscovite'; it lay behind the hostility of the Church and the sects to the 'Antichrist'. which was how the Tsar was described quite early in his reign; and finally opposition extended into Peter's own immediate entourage, gathering round his eldest son, Alexis, who refused to give

73 Peter's Kunstkamera (1718–25) included stuffed elephants and giraffes, and also housed the first open library in Russia

up his old Muscovite way of life, and died of torture in 1718. The death of Alexis showed the world that Peter stood alone, a towering figure on a lonely pinnacle, whose work seemed at first to constitute an episode rather than an epoch. It was, of course, a sign of the strength and logical necessity of his work that it survived this opposition and the period of weak and feeble rulers which followed, and that the next great reformer, Catherine II, managed without much difficulty to consolidate and extend it. For more than two centuries, however, his own people were unable to come to a conclusion about Peter's place in Russian history, uncertain whether to admire or reject him.

Peter began his career as a ruler at the age of seventeen. He at once set his sights towards Europeanization and—very characteristically—first of all in the field of foreign policy, of conquest and expansion towards the sea; this involved shipbuilding and the navy. In particular, he turned to the south, against Turkey, possibly even towards the Dardenelles. Azov was the first prize he won, though it was given up in 1711 and not reconquered until 1774.

He broke off the struggle in order to absorb the experience gained, and to build up his inner resources. With this in view he undertook the journey abroad we have already mentioned. It taught him the methods and principles of European absolutism and mercantilism. Early in his reign he had a medallion struck with the characteristic inscription: 'My position is that of a pupil, and I need teachers.' He was a passionate student, especially of shipbuilding, armaments and industry. His newly acquired knowledge was put into practice immediately, and other young men were sent abroad to pursue similar studies. No Russian before him had ever done anything remotely comparable. The immediate result was to provoke conservative opposition; but this was suppressed with much bloodshed. At the same time his policy of Europeanization began to be put into effect, though at first only in external details such as costume and the shaving of beards.

On his travels he also sought to promote his foreign policy. The most important development, and that which revealed his basic intentions, was his agreement with Augustus the Strong (1697–1733), the ruler of Poland-Saxony, with a view to launching a war

74, 75 The difficult victory at Azov (*left*) helped to convince Peter that he should complete his military education in the West. At Narva in 1704 (*right*) he won decisively on the ground where he had suffered a crushing defeat by the Swedes four years before

against Sweden for the possession of the Baltic coast. He was driven on by the feeling that Russia, both here and in the south, was like 'a man whose sleeves are sewn up'. Determined to break through once and for all, he began the great Nordic War (1700–21) against Charles XII of Sweden, although by no means fully prepared for it. Charles was characterized by Ranke as 'high-minded, simple, immaculate, bold, truthful, God-fearing and unshakeable'; but whilst undoubtedly a brilliant military leader, he was no statesman. Peter, on the other hand, though no hero in battle and no great leader, was a first-class statesman and above all a tough, indefatigable man who learned from his mistakes. His ultimate victory was as significant in eastern Europe as the War of the Spanish Succession (1701–14) in the West.

To begin with, however, the Nordic War left Peter, after the heavy defeat at Narva (1700), in a dangerous position of isolation. Charles XII first overthrew Augustus of Poland-Saxony, then turned against Russia, supported by a revolt in the Ukraine and a treaty with the Hetman Mazeppa. But Peter had used the interval to improve his armaments, and in 1709 he defeated Charles at Poltava.

As Peter realized, it was one of the decisive battles of world history. In his despatch after the battle, he added the characteristic postscript: 'Here the foundation-stone of St Petersburg was laid.' It is true that in the war with the Turks, whom the Swedes had managed to draw into the struggle, Peter found himself, in 1711, in a highly dangerous position, from which he only extricated himself by surrendering Azov, captured earlier. On the other hand, the Baltic provinces now for the most part fell into Peter's hands. Later the struggle for Swedish Pomerania, which he undertook in alliance with Prussia, carried him farther west. He also sought to wrest Finland from Sweden, and defeated the Swedish fleet at Hangöudd in 1714. The fruits of this long struggle were reaped in the Peace of Nystad in 1721. Livonia, Estonia, Ingria (the region in which Petersburg had been founded during the war) and Karelia were annexed by Russia. Sweden's might was destroyed for ever. Through Peter, Russia had become a Baltic power: this was his greatest foreign success.

He also reached out towards the south-east. In a war with Persia he won the west coast of the Caspian Sea, Derben and Baku, in 1723. He had plans for trade in this direction and for a route to India.

76 The greatest of Peter's victories on land was at Poltava in 1709 (*above*). The Tsar is in the centre foreground

77, 78 Charles XII (*above*), Peter's Swedish opponent. An able commander, Charles was swept back by the energy with which Peter animated the vast resources of his State. The medal (*left*) commemorates the Peace of Nystadt which ended the war in 1721 to Peter's entire satisfaction

79 The last major European sea-battle
in which galleys were used
was at Hangöudd,
a Russian victory of 1714

Against Turkey he achieved nothing, but in his campaign he asserted the Russian claim to protect the Christians in the Balkans. Already pan-Slavism was in the air.

Europe felt that Russia's relations with it had changed basically under Peter. Russia was not as yet a full member of the European consortium, but it was fast approaching this status. A sign of this was the adoption in 1721 of the title *imperya*. The ruler of Muscovy became *Emperor of all Russia* and henceforward this title was used in conjunction with the older titles, *tsar* and *gosudar*. The ruling dynasty also formed closer links with European princely society. Peter's nieces married German princes, his son a German princess. In this way the Tsar's family raised itself above the boyars with whom alone it had hitherto intermarried.

Thus Peter, with new methods of diplomacy, military organization, industry and mercantilism, furthered his policy of Europeanization, and approached his ultimate objective. Klyuchevsky has written,

'War was Peter's main instrument, the reform of the army his starting-point, with control of the economy as his ultimate goal'. It was with this in mind, not in order to increase Russia's wealth or raise the level of its civilization and education, that he adopted the absolutism of western Europe, and thus inaugurated a new period in Russian history.

His internal policy was also largely inspired by military considerations. He had no fixed plan and no system. He destroyed a great deal in the old order without replacing it. But his first consideration was the new standing army, the nucleus of which, the Petersburg Guard, was his own creation. Into it he conscripted the nobles as officers and the peasants as soldiers. Both the landowners and the peasant community were now made responsible for supplying recruits. The result was a still heavier burden on the rural population. Peter also introduced a new poll-tax for the maintenance of his army, and once again the peasant community was made jointly responsible for

Раскольникъ говоритъ слушай шырюлышикъ я бороды стрищь не хочю воть п媒ня на тебя скоро караулъ закрю

Цырюлнйикъ хочетъ раскольнику бородѧ стрищь •

80 Regarding the pro-
fuse Russian beard as
an obstacle to progress,
Peter the Great put a
tax on it. Beards be-
came a luxury and
a beard-medal was
worn to prove that the
tax had been paid. The
cartoon shows Peter
as a barber

raising it. All those liable to tax were registered in a 'Revision of Souls', the first of which dates from 1718. This led to an extension of serfdom, which greatly accelerated the process of fusion between the peasantry and the old slave classes.

On the other hand, Peter the Great made few changes in the status of the townspeople, who were in an advantageous position since he depended on them for his commercial and industrial policies. The nobility, however, were inscribed in a new 'table of ranks' arranged in fourteen grades or classes (1722). This system, by which anyone could rise through service into the nobility, first personally and then on an hereditary basis, broke the backbone of the old aristocracy and became a characteristic feature of eighteenth- and nineteenth-century Russia. Peter never called a meeting of the *Zemski Sobor*. The Estates played no rôle in his reign. But under him the social and economic privileges of the non-tax-paying nobility were con-firmed and extended. At the same time, the whole of society was brought within the existing system of compulsory service which became a rigid basis for the social structure right down to 1861.

Every individual and every class was to live not for himself but for the state and the Fatherland.

Peter also strove to bring order into the chaotic political administration. In 1708 he divided the land into provinces (*voyevodstva*), grouped in eight *Gouvernements* (an expression he introduced). At the centre, representing his own authority, he created the Senate (1711) and the so-called 'Colleges' (1718), which can be compared with modern ministries. He also established elected organs of administration. In all cases he attempted to imitate the administrative methods of European absolutism. But the reforms were carried out in the midst of war, and for this reason many were improvised and unsystematic. None the less they were to have important and lasting consequences.

He also forced the Church into his system. The Patriarchate was vacant and he never again filled the office. In its place he set up a state authority, the Most Holy Synod (1721), of which the leading member was a layman, the Chief Procurator. He remained immensely important right down to 1917. The clergy, in short, were to be civil servants just as much as the lay bureaucrats.

81 *The Mice Burying the Cat.* This cartoon, which appeared on Peter's death, long remained popular in Russia. It expresses the resentment of 'Old Russians', 'Old Believers' and other victims of Peter's rule

In relation to all this, Peter's economic policy, chiefly designed to promote manufacturing, and his lively interest in technical and practical matters, as well as in education, were of secondary importance. At the same time he tried, in every field, to impose European ways and methods. His methods were unsystematic but persistent, often senseless though sometimes productive, and he managed his private life in much the same way. He married a Latvian serf and lived quite happily with her (she was later to be Empress Catherine I). His son Alexis, the offspring of his first marriage, he considered incapable of acting as his successor, and condemned him to death because he resisted his father's eagerness for reform. Finally he laid down, in 1722, that the Tsar himself should be free to appoint his own successor, and in this way laid his realm open for a whole century to the evils of an uncertain succession. When he died in 1725 he left behind no one either capable or worthy of succeeding him.

Rough and volcanic, but a man of genius and intuition, working and living only for the state, Peter was the most powerful personality in the history of Russia up to 1917. He towered like a monolith over his age, and it is thus that poets such as Pushkin have portrayed him. He created the mechanism (though not the organism) of the Russia state, and raised Russia to the rank of a great European power. It was he who welded Russia firmly to western Europe. This he did with brutal consistency, and at the cost of vast sacrifices on the part of his people. Side by side with his positive contribution, there is thus a negative aspect to his work. His state was carried on the shoulders of the peasant masses who were increasingly oppressed by war, the nobility and the administration. The tension already existing between the masses and the Tsar, between the forces latent in the people and the demands of the state, a tension which fostered the seeds of revolution, was enormously increased by Peter's activities.

It was only natural that a regression, a period of reaction and sterility should follow these twenty-five years of uninterrupted disturbance. This period lasted until 1762, forty almost fruitless years. There was no real co-ordinated counter-action either by the Estates or by conservative 'old Russian' elements, only the rivalry of aristocratic factions, changes of ruler brought about by violence, *coups d'état*, and government by favourites. The insignificant reigns of Peter's wife, Catherine I (1725–7), and of his grandson Peter II (1727–30), with whom the male Romanov line came to an end, were followed by that of Peter's niece, Anna Ivanovna (1730–40). In Russia her years of rule are traditionally known as a time of government by foreigners, especially by Germans, and for this reason have always been regarded with dislike and hatred. In fact three Germans did hold important offices under this Tsarina: firstly Biron (Bühren), a somewhat trivial character, secondly the brilliant Field-Marshal Münnich, and thirdly the outstanding statesman Ostermann.

During the violent reaction which foreign rule provoked, and in which the Guard played the decisive part, Peter's youngest daughter, Elizabeth (1741–62), came to the throne. Politically her reign was dominated by conservative 'old Russian' ideas, culturally it was strongly influenced by France. Under her, Europeanization was equated with French influence, which soon took a firm hold on the ruling classes, affecting language, education and political attitudes. If the Germans had hitherto been the predominant foreign element, now the French also began to make themselves felt.

In European history, Elizabeth's name is chiefly associated with the Seven Years War, in which she sided against Prussia, whose forces were defeated at Gross-Jägersdorf in 1757, Zorndorf in 1758 and Kunersdorf in 1759. In 1760, Russian troops occupied Berlin. It was, in fact, this war that fused together the eastern and western halves of the European system of states. Without doubt the Russian victories placed Prussia in serious danger. But Russia's participation in the war had little practical purpose, for Elizabeth had no real intention of conquering East Prussia and the Pomeranian coast. In this as in other ways Elizabeth's actions were determined largely by accident, by her own moods and by the changing influences around her. She was undoubtedly a gifted woman; but she was given over to luxury and vice, and unconcerned with matters of state; her reign left no mark on internal affairs. By dying, a childless spinster, at the beginning of 1762, she saved Prussia from certain defeat. For the prince whom she designated as successor was a passionate adherent of Frederick the Great, and immediately made peace with

82 Elizabeth Petrovna, from a medal struck in 1752 on the opening of the new naval yard at Kronstadt. The motto on the reverse reads 'Perficit Parentis Opus'

83 The Fontanka Canal (*opposite* in St Petersburg in 175? The grotto and garden of Elizabeth's Summer Palac are on the righ the private anchorage of th nobility on the le

him. He was the son of her sister, Duchess Anna Petrovna of Holstein-Gottorp, and now ascended the throne as Peter III, the first of the junior line of Romanov-Gottorp, which ruled until 1917. If Tsar Paul was in fact Peter's son, which is often disputed but probably true, it means that no further Russian blood entered the veins of the reigning family. All the Tsars married foreign princesses, usually Germans. Of these, Peter himself was the first. In 1745 he married Princess Sophie of Anhalt-Zerbst who later became the Tsarina Catherine II.

Peter III was probably abnormal. At any rate, as Tsar, he always did the opposite of what necessity dictated. His foreign policy was rendered sterile by his devotion to Prussia, Prussian life and Prussian uniforms. His internal policy was characterized by contempt for anything Russian or Orthodox. He had neither the capacity nor the will to rule. His only domestic measure worth noting was the emancipation of the nobility from the old duty of compulsory service. This duty, which stemmed from the nobility's place in feudal society, was the basis of their rights, and in abolishing it he destroyed their very *raison d'être* and created instead a system of pure privilege enjoyed at the expense of the peasants.

94

Peter III's madness and incompetence soon brought opposition to a head, and his wife Catherine exploited it with great skill. In July 1762 she intrigued with the Guard and had Peter deposed. The way was now open for the second great reign in the history of eighteenth-century Russia.

For some forty years Russia had in effect had no government. The abuses of the court, the unchecked power of the feudal nobility, the corruption of the bureaucracy, and the oppression of the masses had combined to cripple it. Yet Peter the Great's reforms were not undone, in spite of opposition and reaction. Much as people hankered after them, there was no return to the old Muscovite traditions. This indicates how deep-rooted the effects of Peter's achievements were. Moreover, Russia's foreign policy had shown how important its position as a great power had become and how deeply involved it now was in European affairs. This was demonstrated by the active part it played in the war of Polish Succession (1733), by Münnich's campaigns against Turkey in alliance with Austria (1736–9), and by Russian participation in the War of the Austrian Succession (1743–8) and the Seven Years War (1756–62).

In genius, will-power and statesmanlike capacity Catherine II came close to Peter the Great. But her personality was quite unlike his, and she reached the Russian throne from an entirely different milieu. German by birth and foreign to Russian ways, she was called to rule almost entirely by chance. Poorly educated, she developed unaided her aptitude for politics. As Grand-Duchess she had absorbed the ideas of the French Enlightenment, which she helped to propagate in Russia. In 1767 she committed to writing her reflections on politics in her so-called *Nakaz*, the instructions she drew up for a commission preparing a new code of laws. There she set down her belief in reason and progress, in the effectiveness of good laws, in instruction and education, in the goodness of human nature and in the strength of the will. These factors were to be put into operation by popular representation which she wished to grant to the Russian people. She stood for law and the common weal; she desired to influence people's minds and hearts; she was a rationalist and a sentimentalist at the same time. 'What I want', she said, 'is not slavery, but obedience to the law', and she set out to create the necessary conditions for this in Russia.

She adopted Russia as her home and sphere of activity with a remarkable lack of prejudice. Her German origins were entirely suppressed. Intellectually she became French, by nationality and political outlook a Russian. She also managed, with remarkable sureness of touch, to deal with a foreign people so skilfully that, in spite of all her impositions, she aroused its lively enthusiasm.

But no historian can ignore how little was achieved by her reforms, what heavy burdens she laid on the people, how agonizingly the latter, particularly the peasants, reacted against their deteriorating position, and how a régime which began in a spirit of liberal rationalism and optimism ended in reaction and oppression. But these factors do not suffice to define the place of the age of Catherine the Great in Russian history. The mere fact that we speak of an 'age' in connection with Catherine is significant. Peter's influence does not lend itself to the use of this term. He carried through many reforms, but had little formative effect on the spirit of his time. Catherine, on

84 Catherine the Great, by Shubin, 1771 ▶

85, 86, 87 Summit conferences. Catherine meets Gustav III of Sweden after the Russian defeats of 1789–91 (*left*) and Joseph II of Austria on the Dnieper, 1787 (*opposite*). *Below*, Gillray's interpretation of Catherine's motives in 1791. Frustrated in the last of her Turkish wars, she was shortly to be consoled by the new partitions of Poland

QUEEN CATHERINE'S DREAM,

the other hand, caught up in the European political and philosophical movements of her day, introduced them to Russia, or at least to its ruling classes, who became 'enlightened' in the Voltairean or French sense of the word. Furthermore, the new ideas generated new forces and new tensions. They provided a basis for the intellectual developments that took place under Alexander I, and for the controversies between Westernizers and Slavophiles which lasted into the early part of Alexander II's reign. Catherine's influence, in giving these ideas access to her country, illustrates the marked difference between her and Peter the Great, and still more between her and Elizabeth.

Her original aim was simply to restore order and happiness to the Russian people by means of a vast, peaceful process of reform which would have culminated in a 'Europeanization of the spirit'. But she was not strong or consistent enough to carry this through. She could not overcome the reactionary forces around her, to which she soon made great concessions. Still less could she withstand the inherent tendency of the state towards expansion, aggression, war and all the burdens war brought with it. Thus, contrary to her original intentions, foreign affairs were the most important aspect of her programme. In this field she enjoyed considerable success.

Although strongly influenced by sympathies and dislikes in her personal life, in foreign affairs she acted in a cool, Machiavellian manner. She was realistic, consistent and ruthless. She was careful, and did not rely on luck; but her basic policy was definitely one of aggression. She instinctively followed the lines laid down by Peter the Great, in particular his drive towards the sea. Her first objective was Courland.

Having initially remained neutral during the Seven Years War, she then sided with Prussia. Subsequently her foreign policy was conducted in alliance with Austria. But she always retained her freedom of action. During the complications caused by the French Revolution, she kept in the background. Although she agitated against the Revolution and supported the coalition against France, she played no active part, merely exploiting the situation to Russia's advantage, particularly in Poland. This realistic attitude was always an essential feature of her foreign policy. She never allowed herself to be guided by principles, as both her grandsons, Alexander I and Nicholas I, were to do.

After the incorporation of Courland, Catherine pressed on with the annexation of the Baltic coast almost as far as the river Memel and the Prussian border. But she never thought of crossing the border with a view to further conquest. A common interest in the decline of Poland aligned her with Prussia. She had not at first envisaged the partition of Poland; but she had consistently sought to establish a dominant Russian influence in Warsaw, frustrating every Polish attempt at reform or resistance. Turkey's initiation, in 1767, of a war against Russia in Poland's favour, led to the first partition. Austria threatened to enter the war against Russia, because of Russia's successes in Turkey. Prussia, which was allied to Russia, should have come to its aid, but had no wish to, since it had no Near Eastern interests at stake. So as not to endanger its alliance with Prussia, Russia renounced its conquests on the lower Danube, seeking instead a *quid pro quo* in Poland; this Prussia encouraged. Austria had provided the first precedent for the partition of Poland when it occupied part of the country in 1769. And so, in 1772, the first partition of Poland came about. Catherine occupied the White Russian territories on the Dvina and the upper regions of the Dnieper. In 1793 and 1795 the second and third partitions completed the process and Poland disappeared as an independent state. Russia gained some 190,000 square miles in the west, its territory running almost in a straight line from the Baltic to the Black Sea.

The idea of the partition of Poland did not originate with Catherine. It had been under discussion as early as the seventeenth century. But it was she who skilfully exploited circumstances in Russia's favour. It was always her view—on the whole justified—that she had not stolen Polish territory (as Alexander I definitely did in 1815) but had simply reclaimed lands which were historically a part of Russia—in other words, the regions of White and Red Russia. The partition of Poland was, however, an act of barefaced aggression on the part of the three powers involved, and it was Catherine who took the initiative. No doubt Catherine, Frederick II and Maria Theresa were all to blame; but the main responsibility rested on the first two. Poland's internal divisions were also a contributory factor, since they deprived it of the power to defend itself. But although the Polish state disappeared from 1795 to 1916, Polish nationality did not, and the Polish question created difficult problems for Russia and the other partitioning powers.

Catherine's second sphere of success in foreign policy was the Near East. Turkey was thought to be as near to collapse as Poland, and its partition was openly discussed. For Russia this opened up the prospect of obtaining Bessarabia, the so-called Danube Principalities (Moldavia and Wallachia), control of the Black Sea, Constantinople and the Dardanelles, and a protectorate over the Christian peoples of the Balkans, who longed for deliverance from Turkey. These were the aims which Catherine sought to put into effect in her Turkish wars. She also had other, more far-fetched plans, such as the establishment of an Empire in the Balkans under a Russian Grand Duke.

She waged two wars against Turkey, in 1767–74 and 1787–92. The first brought the naval victory in the Straits of Chios (1770) and ended in 1774 with the Peace of Kuchuk-Kainarji, by which Azov was united with Russia, the Tartars were made independent of Turkey (and so ready for subjugation by Russia), and Russia acquired a kind of protectorship over the Christians in Turkey. The second Turkish war ended with the Peace of Jassy (1792), by which Russia secured the region between the Bug and the Dniester.

Probably the most important acquisition during this period, however, was the Crimea (1783). Catherine's famous journey to southern Russia in 1787 in company with her favourite, Potemkin, gave notice to the rest of Europe of Russia's new position on the Black Sea. Odessa was founded in 1794. It developed quickly as a centre for the export trade in grain which had grown considerably since the middle of the century.

Catherine's war with Persia was less important, but it was of significance for the future and extended the Russian sphere of influence to Transcaucasia and Georgia (1796).

88 Count Rumantsev's victory over the Turks on the Kagul River, 1770

89 Grigory Potemkin had taken a modest part in the *coup* of 1762 and distinguished himself with Rumantsev against the Turks before he caught Catherine's fancy in 1774. He remained influential in her councils until his death in 1791

The extent to which Russia's standing in Europe had changed was shown at the Peace of Teschen (1779), when Catherine acted as mediator between Prussia and Austria. To a far greater degree than Peter I, she had made Russia into an influential member of the European consortium. She was also able to take advantage of the conflicts of the other powers to expand south and west, and even at that time there were people who saw Russia's growing power as a menace. Catherine's successes were, indeed, the basis for the decisive rôle in European affairs which Russia was to play between 1813 and 1815. They also brought the Empress great renown. But from a Russian point of view they had adverse consequences which cannot be overlooked. The progress achieved in the north and south was probably advantageous; that in the centre, at the expense of Poland, was more disputable. More important, Catherine's successes in foreign affairs diverted her attention from the situation within Russia which required far more care than she was able to give it.

Catherine's domestic policy—to confine ourselves to its positive aspects—had three landmarks:

1. In 1767 she summoned a Commission of representatives of all the Estates and nationalities to draw up a new code of laws. She shared the conviction—so characteristic of the Enlightenment's belief in reason—that good laws guarantee progress, and she

103

herself drew up an 'Instruction' for the Commission, which she had printed in four languages. Her action in voluntarily calling together the Estates caused a sensation in Europe, but it showed little sense of reality. How did she think that hundreds of people, differing in character and outlook, could possibly compile a new code of laws? In fact, the Commission was disbanded after a few years, having achieved nothing.

2. In 1775 she re-organized the administrative structure. She increased the number of *Gouvernements* from eight to fifty, which were subdivided into districts. This structure, which was expanded as the Empire grew in size, lasted till the end of the Romanov period. Under the Soviet régime it was replaced by regional divisions based on economic and national factors.

3. In 1785 she promulgated charters of privilege, granting the nobility and the townspeople a kind of self-government. This meant little to the towns, considering the backwardness of the *bourgeoisie* in Russia at that time. The assemblies of the nobility,

90, 91, 92 Impressions of life in the suburbs of St Petersburg *c.* 1768 show the roofing of a log house, and vendors of live fish and sturgeons' eggs. The view taken by A. N. Radishchev (*right*) was less romantic

on the other hand, which were established in both the districts and the *Gouvernements* to carry out certain administrative tasks, though not in fact real organs of self-government, fulfilled many of its functions. So the real importance of these charters was in strengthening the influence of the nobility.

This was reflected in the depression of the peasantry. It was under Catherine that the system of serfdom, which lasted until 1861, was finally consolidated. The peasants were now literally chattels, an oppressed and exploited mass without rights. There were even instances in her reign of the sale of peasants without the land to which they were attached—in other words, pure slave-trading—although the practice was forbidden by law. The glaring contradiction between the Empress's fine theories and the sordid reality was revealed in Radishchev's famous book, *A Journey from St Petersburg to Moscow*, written in 1790. It was the first important literary account of the sufferings of the peasants, and as such is of lasting significance. The liberal Tsarina condemned the author to death, but reprieved

93 The Easter festival in Podnovinsky Square in Moscow, 1796. The common people enjoy the amusements of the fair, including the *balançoires* characteristic of Russia, while the gentry circulate in carriages

him and banished him to Siberia. His little book was suppressed. Not until 1905 could it be published in an unabridged form.

Catherine also extended the area of peasant oppression. She introduced serfdom into White Russia and the Ukraine, where it was not yet fully developed. As a result of her innumerable gifts of land and serfs to her favourites, moreover, conditions among the peasants deteriorated still further. In the end, the old peasant unrest, exacerbated by a régime which became more reactionary as time went on, led to a revolt in the south-east of the Empire, which, on account of its violence and horror, remained imprinted for decades on the minds of the Russian ruling class. It was led by a Cossack, Emelyan Ivanovich Pugachev, who claimed to be Peter III, Catherine's murdered husband, much as the false Dmitri had entered upon the scene in an earlier age. He conquered and laid waste vast areas. The insurrection lasted from 1773 to 1775, and besides involving the peasants, was the last rising of the Cossacks as a free race. But it was ruthlessly put down and Pugachev was publicly executed in Moscow in January 1775.

94 Emelyan Pugachev (*above*)
claimed to be Peter III
fighting for his rights against
a wicked and usurping wife.
Catherine had him
exhibited in chains
and publicly quartered
in Red Square in 1775

95, 96 Posters making use of
an either-or method to
advertise smallpox inoculation,
introduced into Russia
at the end
of Catherine's reign

Catherine's reversion to a reactionary policy and the intensification of serfdom coincided with an increase in the commercial interests of the nobility, which had been growing stronger since about 1750. Russia had come to be regarded as Europe's granary and the nobility was increasingly interested in grain exports, especially to England. Not surprisingly, their interests carried more weight than Catherine's early liberalism. In fact, Catherine capitulated to the landed classes. The alliance between the monarchy, the nobility, the corps of officers and the bureaucracy was the dominant factor, and the peasantry—that is, the vast majority of the people—were held down in misery and bondage. Under her, the old contradiction between success abroad and misery at home continued unabated. In a reign of thirty-four years, seventeen were years of war.

Catherine's brilliant court and her intellectual activities should not be allowed to obscure these facts. From the outside the Russian Empire was a splendid edifice; within, it was riddled by disorder, misery and corruption. She brought to their logical conclusion the developments which made the clergy into servants of the state, and she appropriated the Church's property. Her interest in the Enlightenment did not extend to the people. There was, for example, no systematic policy of popular education. On the other hand, the upper classes—'society' in the narrower sense—were profoundly affected. She converted the court, which had been hitherto backward, if not barbaric, into a centre of culture. She gave it access to the European civilization of the period, to its freedom of thought and its scepticism. Her reign saw the beginning of a great literary movement, as well as advances in science and in art. There is no doubt that these achievements gave a major impetus to Russian national self-consciousness. 'Since the time of Peter the Great', in Klyuchevsky's words, 'the Russians had hardly dared call themselves human beings. In the reign of Catherine they considered themselves not only human beings, but a people of the first rank in Europe.'

But we must not forget the reactionary elements behind the brilliance, culture and artistry of the court. In particular, the Europeanization of the upper classes led to a deep and long-lasting estrangement between them and the people. Neither understood the other any longer. The Tsarina was a stranger to her subjects, and a new kind of tension grew up between the state and the ordinary people. Catherine's reign strongly accentuated this. Right down to 1917, the rift on the spiritual plane between the upper classes and the masses was never healed. In the end it was one of the main causes of the Great Revolution.

Even so, Catherine II is still one of the greatest women ever to have occupied a throne, and her reign one of the greatest in the whole of Russian history. What a fascinating picture she presents! The insignificant princess from a commonplace Prussian officer's family, with little education or refinement, thrust into an alien environment, full of brilliance and barbarism, vice and intrigue, and into a marriage fraught with tensions and dangers; ambitious, sensual, driven by her lust for power to overthrow her husband, ascend the throne of the Tsars, and lead Russia for a whole generation! A multitude of discordances and contradictions marked her reign and for that reason no straightforward assessment of it is possible. But her 'enlightened absolutism' was an important factor in Russian history.

Charming and domineering, Catherine was able to secure the co-operation of great statesmen and generals, and direct their activities; and they for their part all admired her. At the same time, with her many lovers and favourites (amongst whom Potemkin was the most important), she led a self-indulgent, profligate life, which popular history has often treated as though it were the only thing that mattered about her. In fact, whatever we may think about her private life, it was never of real importance, and she did not allow herself to be swamped by it. Her favourites were not permitted to take part in the business of state, and she kept dissipation out of her politics. At all events, her statesmanship was her most important quality. To a greater degree than any other woman in modern history she was a statesman at heart, and yet she retained her feminine qualities.

Catherine was succeeded by her son Paul I (1796–1801), whose only object was to do the opposite to his mother, and whose reign was merely an interlude. He inherited all his father's instability and acted always in a wilful, despotic manner. He wanted peace and yet waged war in alliance with England and Austria against revolutionary France. Although this campaign (1799) was marked by the brilliant generalship of Suvorov in northern Italy and in Switzerland, it had no obvious connexion with Russian interests. Shortly afterwards, Paul allied himself with Napoleon against England and planned a joint attack on India. His home policy was equally arbitrary, infuriating and harming the nobility. In the end, their opposition to his reign of terror resulted in a conspiracy in which Paul was assassinated. He was followed by his sons Alexander I and Nicholas I in succession.

Alexander I (1801–25) was the most outstanding of the Romanov-Gottorps who followed Catherine II. He is also the most complicated and difficult to assess. Historians have usually considered him weak and easily influenced. In fact, he was fundamentally a strong man, but reserved and impenetrable, forever acting a part, which, if it deceived others, never deceived himself. More a sentimentalist than

a rationalist, his early tendency towards liberalism was succeeded by leanings towards mysticism. Yet, the enlightened liberal education he received from his Swiss tutor, Frédéric-César Laharpe, left its mark. He wanted to give his people peace and happiness, to reform the country, to free the peasants and to frame a constitution. But, like his predecessors, he was drawn into foreign politics and war, which filled the first half of his reign, and in the second half he reverted to reactionary policies, allowing the country to return to a state of disorder.

By Alexander's time Russia's place in Europe was such that the Tsar became a leader in the wars against the French Revolution and Napoleon. Indeed, it is hardly too much to say that the part he played in the struggle against French hegemony made Alexander in effect the first ruler of Europe. The conflict began soon after his accession when he declared war on Napoleon, in alliance with England, Austria and Prussia. The first phase lasted until 1807 and from a Russian point of view was far from successful. Napoleon defeated the Austrians and the Russians at Austerlitz in 1805. In 1807 the Russians were defeated at Friedland, and at the Peace of Tilsit in the same year Alexander abandoned Prussia. But no great damage had been done to Russia, and he quickly reversed his policy.

97, 98 Napoleon and the Tsar Alexander I meet in mid-river at Tilsit in 1807 (*opposite*). *Right*, the victorious Tsar in 1815

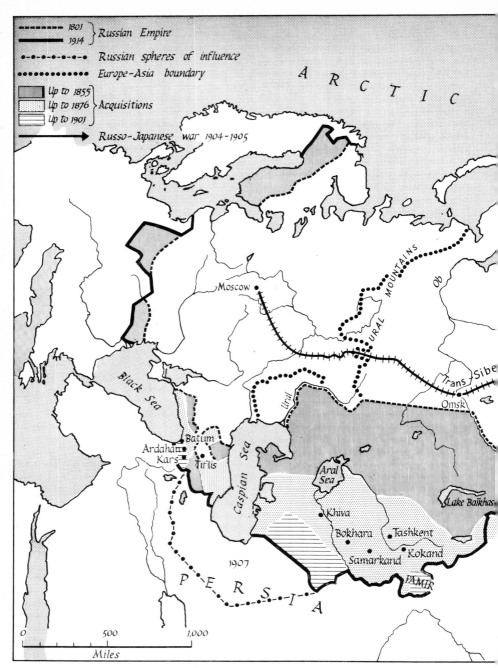

99 Russian expansion in Asia, 1800–1914

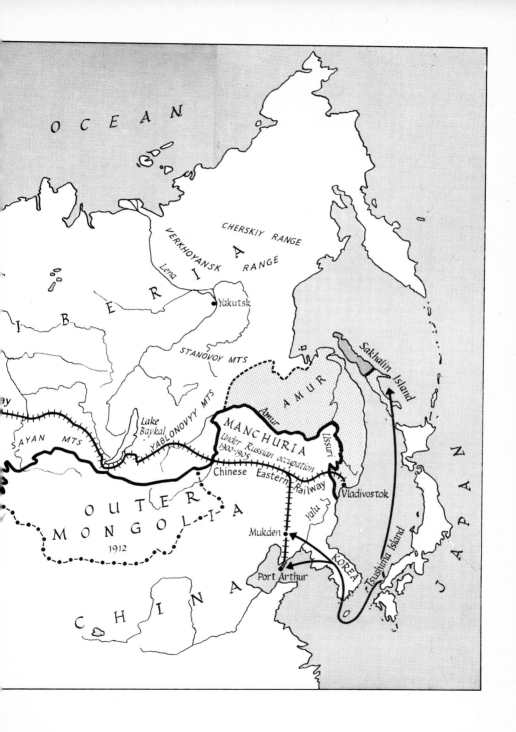

O C E A N

S I B E R I A

CHERSKIY RANGE

VERKHOYANSK RANGE

Lena

•Yakutsk

STANOVOY MTS

AMUR

Amur

Sakhalin Island

SAYAN MTS

Lake
Baykal

YABLONOVYY MTS

MANCHURIA
Under Russian occupation
1900-1905

Lissuri

Chinese Eastern Railway

Vladivostok

O U T E R
M O N G O L I A
1912

Yalu

Mukden

JAPAN

Port Arthur

KOREA

Tsushima Island

C H I N A

100 Moscow burning, 14 September 1812, as Napoleon's cavalry arrive in the Kremlin

In the second phase, from 1808 to 1812, France and Russia were, in appearance at least, allies. Instead of fighting Napoleon, Alexander's intention now was to divide the world with him. But economic factors soon caused a rift in their alliance. When Napoleon introduced the continental blockade against England and sought to involve Russia in the scheme through the Berlin decree of 1806, the opposition of the landowners, who were vitally interested in the export trade, made it impossible for Alexander to participate. Nevertheless, he skilfully used the period of peace with France to further Russia's political interests. First of all, he made war on Sweden, and acquired the Grand Duchy of Finland in 1809 at the Peace of Frederikshamm. In the same year, at the diet of Borgo, he demanded autonomy for the rest of Finland and established the union between the two countries which was to last until shortly before the First World War. Then he declared war on Turkey and Persia, winning Bessarabia from the former at the Peace of Bucharest in 1812, and Baku from the latter at the Peace of Gulistan in 1813. If this territorial expansion is to be regarded as a gain, Russia's debt to Alexander is obvious; but it should be noted that the lands he acquired were no longer former Russian territories won back for the

Fatherland, as earlier conquests had been, but non-Russian territories inhabited by non-Russian peoples who were subjugated by Russia.

By this time the conflict between Alexander and Napoleon was on the point of being re-opened. Its final phase began in June 1812, when the latter crossed the Memel and set foot on Russian territory. One hundred and twenty-nine years later, almost to the day, Hitler launched his attack on Russia. For both it was the great turning-point in their careers. Hitler did not reach Moscow; Napoleon succeeded in occupying it, but the occupied city went up in flames. Though the fire was probably accidental, it compelled Napoleon to retreat, and the retreating troops were harried until the straggling remnants of the Grand Army limped back across the Russian frontier. For the Russians the war of 1812 was a great patriotic war, which stirred national feeling in much the same way as the German invasion in 1941. It was not the generals or the statesmen who were the heroes but—as Tolstoy later brought out so graphically in his great novel *War and Peace*—the Russian people themselves. They, Russia's vast expanses and the Russian winter were the forces that defeated Napoleon's *Grande Armée*.

101 *Review of the French Troops at Smolensk* in full retreat, 1812, as drawn by Cruikshank after the Russian cartoonist Terebenev

As the French retreated, Alexander advanced into central and western Europe. Here, a historic decision faced him. If he had only considered Russian interests, he might have stopped short at the Niemen. Instead, under the influence of Stein, he pressed on in alliance with England, Prussia and Austria until final victory was won. The Tsar, as champion of Europe, had Napoleon as his deadly enemy. He was determined, he said, 'to destroy this abomination' and 'to crush the serpent's head'. It was not desire for conquest as such that drove him on but the will to destroy the despotism of one man, and so establish a balance of power that should liberate Europe from French hegemony. From the campaigns of 1813 to the final entry into Paris in March 1814, Alexander relentlessly pursued his aim. He also played a vital part in the first and second Peace of Paris and in the re-organization of Europe at the Congress of Vienna.

In Russia, as a result of his successes, Alexander was called 'the Blessed'. He had, without doubt, greatly expanded the Russian Empire. In addition, the Polish question was settled by what amounted to a fourth partition. It was not a settlement which entirely conformed with Alexander's wishes; but on the whole it satisfied the interests of Russia, which acquired the district around the middle reaches of the Vistula (including Warsaw). Russian territory now projected westwards like a wedge, beyond a line running north and south from Torun to Cracow, in defiance of Prussia. Thus Russia's foothold in central Europe was considerably strengthened and the link between its Baltic territory and its sphere of influence in the south-east was forged more rigidly than necessity dictated. In exchange the Tsar had acquired subjects in Poland who were hostile to Orthodox Christianity and violently anti-Russian. Alexander sought to overcome the resultant problems by giving the Poles of the Duchy of Warsaw internal autonomy. A similar policy was pursued in Finland. But although the Duchy of Warsaw had its own constitution from 1815 to 1830, the Polish question was not solved.

At Vienna, Alexander aimed at more than a territorial re-organization of Europe. Sickened by years of war, impelled by his own mystico-religious nature, he desired in all sincerity to establish a lasting peace. This was the basis of the Holy Alliance (26 September

1815), by which he tried to unite the monarchs (but not the peoples) 'in the name of the higher truths which are established by the eternal laws of God the redeemer'. In other words, he hoped to ensure eternal peace through co-operation between the monarchs, and to rule his subjects like the father of a family. The others smiled at such sentimental day-dreaming, and in fact the Holy Alliance achieved virtually nothing. Moreover, Alexander himself soon ceased to act according to his principles. As his opposition to anything even faintly revolutionary or liberal grew stronger, the Holy Alliance became simply a tool for oppression and reaction.

Alexander's policy at home also became more and more reactionary. His immersion in European politics and the intervention of the war years prevented the fruition of his early plans for liberal reform. With the aid of a really creative statesman, Mikhail Mikhailovich Speransky, he made a number of administrative innovations— e.g. the Council of State (in 1810) and the Ministries (1802–11)— which lasted until 1917. But a new balance between legislation, administration, the courts of law, the ruler and popular assembly, such as Speransky had envisaged, was prevented by opposition from the ruling nobility. There is no doubt that at one time he had seriously considered the emancipation of the peasantry; but no more than Catherine II before him, or his brother Nicholas later, was he able to override the opposition of the land-owning nobility. Not even an autocracy as powerful as his could do this.

Nothing was done to alter the situation within the country. Serfdom continued to be its characteristic feature. Demands from the landowners continued to weigh heavily on the peasants, and their position deteriorated as a result of the exigencies of long wars and the demands of government.

By now an active opposition was developing in Russia. Its sources were twofold. On the one side there was the conservative 'old Russia' faction, which derived its strength from the nationalism revived by the war, and decried all liberal tendencies in the Emperor. On the other side was the liberal opposition. A considerable number of young officers among the nobility had come into contact with Western ideas (Enlightenment, Rationalism, Natural Law, Liberalism,

Representation of the People, Democracy) during the French wars, since when these ideas had spread fairly widely. The French *avant-garde* no longer supported the régime as they had done in the time of Catherine II. Westernization now tended to produce revolutionary tendencies, resistance to absolutism, and demands for a modern system of government in Russia, based on the western European model. This was reflected not merely by the ideas of a few outstanding writers, but also by the attitude of considerable numbers of young nobles and officers who were already organizing secret societies and conspiracies. The result was the famous revolt of the army and nobility, the Decembrist rising, which broke out in 1825 immediately after Alexander's death. This was the first revolutionary movement with stated political objectives in Russian history, totally different in character from the spontaneous peasant risings of earlier centuries.

How are we to sum up the reign of Alexander I? Taken as a whole it has an important place in Russian history, though its domestic results were negligible, if not positively harmful. In his foreign policy, Alexander was certainly not simply a conqueror or a Russian imperialist. His war against Napoleon was waged not only in the interests of Russia, but with the object of emancipating Europe from Napoleonic despotism. At the Congress of Vienna, Alexander and the other statesmen present founded an international system which lasted for decades and established Russia's predominance on the continent of Europe. This was not only significant for Russia. But the increase in his external power resulted in a catastrophic change in Alexander's character. The terrible experiences of the year 1812, in particular, provoked a spiritual turmoil which drove him from liberalism to mysticism and reaction. Basically a gentle and humane man, he became more and more distrustful and reserved; and as he grew old and weary, he lost his inner equilibrium. He died in 1825 a dissatisfied and broken man. Popular legend had it that he withdrew to Siberia where he lived for many years as a hermit under a false name. The legend was false; but it showed what this complicated and enigmatic individual was thought capable of doing.

102 The Decembrists. From left to right, Pavel Pestel (executed 1826), S. Maravyev-Apostol, whose regiment, the Chernigov, supported the abortive revolution, A. Bestuzhov, P. Kakhovsky and K. Ryleyev

Alexander I left the empire in a state of great confusion, riddled with conspiracies of which he even seems to have been unaware. He had no sons and the succession was uncertain. According to the law promulgated by his father, Paul I, the next in succession should have been Constantine, the elder of the two surviving brothers. Constantine, however, had renounced his claim to the throne, and Alexander had therefore decreed that Nicholas, his younger brother, should succeed. But his decision had been kept secret and great confusion arose before Nicholas finally assumed the title of Emperor. The officers already conspiring in Petersburg and elsewhere took advantage of this unexpected opportunity to strike. But the revolt was neither sufficiently widespread nor adequately prepared. On the morning of 26 December 1825 a few units refused to take the oath of allegiance to Nicholas. Fighting broke out in the square outside the Senate House in Petersburg, where the great memorial to Peter the Great stands, but the Tsar was an easy victor. The rising was suppressed, and many arrests followed.

119

The significance of the Decembrists, as they were called, lies not so much in their revolt as such, which failed, as in the liberal political programme they sought to implement. Their rising marks the beginning of the conscious revolutionary movement which culminated in 1917, and is usually treated as part of that movement. For the time being, however, Nicholas I was complete master of the situation, and for the ensuing thirty years, from 1825 to 1855, he ruled unchallenged.

In Nicholas I the absolutism of Petersburg was firmly re-established, until it was shaken to its foundations by the Crimean War.

A simple man with none of his brother's complexity nor his tendency to liberalism and his mystical streak, Nicholas felt no need to base his government on abstract theory. He was satisfied with the established threefold doctrine of Autocracy, Orthodoxy and Nationalism. This programme, which prevailed for the rest of the nineteenth century, was a simple one, yet it led to considerable developments. As its basis it had the two traditional Muscovite dogmas, Tsarism and Orthodoxy; but these were now reinforced—significantly enough—by the new element of Russian Nationalism.

103 The Imperial Cuirassiers, jewels of an autocratic crown, in 1850

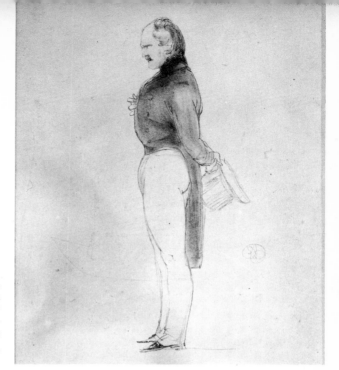

104 Tsar Nicholas I, a lithograph from the study by Landseer issued at the Tsar's death in 1855

Nor was there anything novel about Nicholas's domestic policy. It was limited, naïve and hard to the point of cruelty. In this it was characteristic of a ruler who, on the surface, was majestic, self-sufficient and awe-inspiring. Despotic at home and an opponent of all revolutionary tendencies abroad, Nicholas sought to insulate Russia against all possible forms of contagion from the West. With that in view he suppressed freedom of thought and freedom of conscience. His secret police enforced a sterile régime of terror. He believed that his iron determination to maintain the *status quo* was enough, and he tried to convince himself of his success by tours of inspection throughout the empire. Towards the end of his reign, how-ever, he could no longer avoid perceiving that what he saw on these tours was carefully pre-arranged, and that, for all his interference, he had not really achieved anything. His whole reign was marked by oppression and regimentation, which it is unnecessary to describe in detail. The literature of the period is full of passages which portray current conditions, though the writers often had to confine

121

themselves to hints and innuendoes on account of the censorship. Nicholas I had been called the Don Quixote of absolutism. His attitude did much to hasten the growth of the revolutionary movement.

Nicholas did nothing to promote the welfare of the country. The rapid development of early capitalism which occurred in his reign was not initiated by him. It is true that he was genuinely interested in agrarian reform, but his measures only affected the peasants on the imperial domains. Those on private estates, who constituted the vast majority, remained in misery. Meanwhile, ideas of emancipation were making headway and local peasant risings, which revealed the terrible condition of the people, continued to occur. Nicholas's policy of 'Russification', the expression of a growing nationalism, also added to the internal tension. 'Russification' led to conflict between the Great Russian majority and the other nationalities of the Empire, including the Little Russians, the Poles, the Jews and the Germans. It was directed against foreign languages and religions, which were attacked in the interests of uniformity. In fact, it was a utopian and unrealistic policy, serving only to increase the general confusion. It created new centres of unrest among the downtrodden nationalities and so multiplied the seeds of revolution in Russia. The state of the national finances also contributed to the general state of unrest and instability. Loans multiplied and the currency was devalued by the issue of paper money. Another important factor was the burden imposed by Nicholas's costly foreign policy; but how could Russia hope to compete with a Europe which was striding ahead in wealth and technical attainments, while its whole political and social structure was left to stagnate?

Nicholas's foreign policy, in fact, was contradictory and inconsistent. His first objective was the negative one of warding off the revolutionary changes which had taken place in the rest of Europe. But at the same time he adopted an aggressive attitude towards the 'Eastern question'. He spread his net ever wider, reaching out to the Danubian Principalities and the Dardanelles, and planning the partition of Turkey and the establishment of a protectorate over the Balkan peoples. In all these directions his policy was expansive and tinged with a pan-Slav ideology. But if he failed to appreciate the contradictions in his own policy, he was even less aware of the shift that had taken place in the international situation. By now the Western powers were no longer prepared to view Russia's advance with indifference, and felt that their own interests were threatened. This applied first and foremost to England, to a lesser extent to France and Austria. Nicholas had the illusory idea that he could simultaneously act as Europe's mandatary and serve the interests of Russia. In fact, they were irreconcilable objectives.

Nicholas's first campaign was against Persia. Its object was to free the Caucasus from Persian control, and it was concluded by the Peace of Turkmanchai in 1828, by which Russia acquired the region on the left bank of the Araxes and the city of Erivan. This campaign was followed by a war with Turkey (1828–9), the purpose of which was to acquire Transcaucasia—in other words, Georgia and Armenia. This would provide a base from which to subdue the mountainous country stretching from Georgia to the Kuban and Terek regions which were already in Russian hands. The war with Turkey was brought to an end by the Peace of Adrianople in 1829. It secured for Russia the left bank of the lower Danube and the islands at its mouth, the east coast of the Black Sea, the city and province of Akhaltsikhe in Georgia, and certain concessions with regard to the Straits. But though the war ended successfully for Russia, it brought tangible proofs of the previously mentioned change of attitude on the part of the Western powers. In face of their opposition it was, in fact, only the mediation of Prussia that rescued Nicholas from a difficult situation. Moreover, it was also clear that Russia was too weak internally to wage a major campaign, and the war with Turkey undoubtedly overtaxed its resources. Nevertheless, by the Treaty of Unkiar-Skelessi (1833), Nicholas secured control of the Straits and a virtual protectorate over Turkey. The Sultan closed the Bosphorus and the Dardanelles to the warships of all other countries and became Russia's ally. But the Great Powers soon forced Nicholas to retreat. As early as 1840, Russia was forced to share its protectorate over Turkey with England, Austria, France and Prussia, and from that time on, although it made many attempts to restore its position, its say in the 'Eastern question' declined.

In his policy towards Europe, Nicholas saw himself as the protector of legitimism and the restoration, and as the Continent's appointed guardian against revolution. This was the purpose for which he used the power Russia had acquired in the wars against Napoleon. When, after the 1830 revolution in France, revolt broke out in Russian Poland, Nicholas crushed the rising, abrogated the Polish constitution, and reduced the Kingdom of Poland, as constituted in 1815, to the status of a Russian province. He saw the Poles as a dangerous revolutionary force, in close contact both with the opposition in Russia and with the revolutionary movements in Europe, and he therefore intensified his anti-revolutionary policy in alliance with Austria and Prussia. He was not the cleverest member of the anti-revolutionary alliance—the Austrian statesman Metternich was far superior in this respect—but he was the strongest, and was therefore feared and hated by all liberal and revolutionary forces in Europe. For them he was *the* enemy.

In 1846 there was a new Polish rising, this time in Austrian Poland. When in 1848 the revolution which had broken out in France spread to Austria and Prussia, Nicholas came to their aid in full force. In 1849 his armies overthrew the rising in Hungary. But his main aim was to support his brother-in-law, Frederick William IV of Prussia, and prevent him from making concessions to the German liberals and nationalists. This was achieved in 1850 at Olmütz when Prussia acceded to Russia's demands. Between 1850 and 1854, Nicholas was the effective master of continental Europe. Only England stood apart; between her and Russia there were, as yet, few real points of dispute. It was Nicholas himself who provoked the hostility of England. Carried away by his new pre-eminence, he thought that the other powers would stand passively aside while he took over the inheritance of the 'sick man of Europe', Turkey. It was a grave miscalculation, which resulted in the Crimean War and led to a severe crisis in Russia. The Crimean War was the first such major conflict since 1815. England, France and Italy fought on the side of Turkey, and Austria also joined the Western alliance, though it did not actually take part in the fighting. Even so, Vienna's decision to throw in its weight on Turkey's side was the beginning of the hostility

105 The siege of Sevastopol, 1854

between Russia and Austria which was one of the main causes of the First World War, and of the collapse of the two empires.

The Peace of Paris, which brought the Crimean War to an end, was not signed until after Nicholas's death. The war itself was inconclusive. The Western powers attacked wherever they could, but they had little hope of destroying the Russian colossus, since they were unable to launch a direct land attack from Prussia or Austria. Hence the fighting on land was confined to the Crimea, where the main action was the siege of Sevastopol. During the siege, which lasted from October 1854 to September 1855, a total of 350 days, Nicholas died. He died a broken and despairing man, for the Russian defeats had shown him that the autocratic system and the army on which it rested had failed to meet the demands made upon it. Shortly before his death he said to his successor: 'I am not handing over the command in the good order I should have wished, and I am bequeathing you much worry and distress.' This understatement was a confession that the whole system of absolute government, as it had evolved during the Petersburg period, had ended in bankruptcy.

The Crimean War did not shake Russia as much as the Russo-Japanese War and the First World War were to do. Even so, it was of epoch-making significance. In Europe, Russia's power was seriously weakened. At home criticism, disaffection and revolutionary tendencies grew apace. Not only the Tsar but also the ruling classes —that is to say, the nobility, the officers' corps and the bureaucracy —lost confidence. It was evident that the Russian state was far less powerful than they had thought. The army, the administration, the finances and the system of communications had all proved inadequate, and all Russia's social and economic weaknesses were exposed. The Crimean War opened wide the way to revolution, for which economic developments had already prepared the ground. This was the situation in which Nicholas I's reign ended. For long, popular legend had it that he committed suicide in a fit of despair. Europe heaved a sigh of relief at the news of his death, liberated at last from the nightmare which his power had conjured up. A fresh start was clearly needed; and people waited eagerly to see in what direction Russia and the new Tsar would move.

106 The Redan, one of the outworks of Sevastopol, after the Russian retreat in September 1855

107 Chair in cut steel
made at the Tula foundry
in the late
eighteenth century

INTERNAL DEVELOPMENTS IN RUSSIA (1689–1855)

If we compare conditions in Russia from Peter the Great to Nicholas with those in western Europe, it is evident that both were in a process of economic transformation, though Russia lagged far behind. Russian historians have emphasized that during this period the same influences were at work there as in the rest of Europe, but they were modified by circumstances and their effects were felt later. In Russia, as elsewhere, there existed around 1800 a mercantilist system ender state control. The local small-scale crafts could no longer meet the needs of the administration, whose requirements in the military field grew rapidly from the time of Peter the Great. Under Peter, mercantilist policies were more extensively, though still somewhat unsystematically, applied. Factories were set up—not yet, of course, machine factories, but workshops which employed large numbers of workers in one place on one task. They mainly served the administration, but some were private, and labour was recruited by the simple process of drafting serfs into them. In this way the textile industry, the iron-works of the Urals, and similar undertakings were established. Already by the eighteenth century their importance was considerable, but they were not capitalist undertakings in the ordinary sense of the word.

108 Russian landed proprietors gambling with bundles of serfs as stakes, by Gustave Doré, 1854

True, certain forms of capitalism had been in existence in Russia from a very early stage. It is possible to describe the early commercial exchanges between Kiev and Constantinople as capitalist, in so far as they implied buying up raw materials and trading them for profit, as well as the use of money and a system of credit. But the trade with Constantinople was largely a trade in luxury goods, not food and other staple products, and it did not result in the production of capital goods. On the whole, therefore, it is more correct to call it pre-capitalist. Moreover, in the succeeding period this commerce tended to decline. Compared with Kiev, Moscow was geographically somewhat remote from the trade-routes to Constantinople and the Mediterranean and its economy tended to revert to a more primitive state. In the Muscovite period there was, of course, an urban population with commercial interests. But the break-up of Russia into a number of principalities meant that, instead of a single economy covering the whole country, there was a series of small, separate economic units, each with its own domestic industries and crafts.

109 Merchants of Novgorod drinking tea. A photograph taken towards the end of the nineteenth century

Such industry as there was, in short, was localized, and it was only when the Tsars, from the time of Ivan III, began to 'reassemble' the Russian lands, that an economic system covering the whole of Russia slowly came into being.

Capitalism in Russia may be said to date from the third or fourth decades of the nineteenth century, even though it existed in embryo from as early as the 1770s. It was only then that a considerable part, though still not the majority, of the labour force was engaged in capitalist enterprise, and that capitalist industry began to cater for a number of basic needs. Napoleon I's continental blockade was an important factor in stimulating Russian industry. A powerful capitalist element had also developed as a consequence of the export trade in grain. The export of grain had, of course, been a factor prior to that, but after the end of the Seven Years War it made immense strides and began to influence the whole economic system. Indeed, it would be hard to exaggerate its importance during the period between the beginning of the nineteenth century and the

110, 111 Views of mid-Victorian St Petersburg. The gardens of the first Summer Palace (*left*). Russia's first railway, from the royal town of Pavlovsk to St Petersburg, seen (*right*) at Tsarskoye Selo, 1830.

First World War. According to Pokrovsky, Russia exported almost seven million *pood* of grain (wheat) in 1801, twice as much in 1820, almost three times as much in 1840 and 26 million *pood* in 1850 (one *pud* equals 35 pounds). England was the main purchaser, paying for its imports with industrial goods. From 1850, the consequences of this export trade became increasingly apparent from decade to decade. It resulted, in particular, in the imposition of a still heavier burden of forced labour on the peasants, and led to conflicts between the different capitalist interests.

Unfortunately we have no adequate statistics of production and output during the early capitalist period in Russia. But it is clear that, from the time of Peter the Great, the growth of the armaments industry was uninterrupted. The demands on it were increased by the wars of Catherine II and Alexander I and by the Turkish War of 1828–9, though the Crimean War showed that even by then they were far from adequately met. Military requirements also constituted a powerful incentive to develop the textile and metallurgical industries. But if government commissions gave the main impetus to the growth of industrial capitalism, private enterprise also played its part, and finance was stimulated by the needs of a

112 The Neva warehouse for foreign goods, *Gostinny Dvor* (*above*), was designed in the 1720s by Tressini. The Tsar's Custom House is visible in the left background

state which was nearly always at war. The pursuit of an ambitious foreign policy by a country with a backward economy necessitated recourse to foreign loans and credit; and there is no doubt that the impact of foreign capitalism hastened developments in Russia. But so long as there was no system of unfettered wage-earning labour, it was impossible to achieve a fully-fledged capitalist system. The old-fashioned structure, in which the employees in factories and mills were serfs bound to the land, was patently inadequate, and new methods of production were frustrated so long as this was the only form of labour available.

This was the factor that limited the growth of capitalism, down to the middle of the nineteenth century. By the reign of Nicholas I, the interests of the nobility and capitalists called for the emancipation of the peasants which alone could make further progress possible. In fact, this development did not get under way until the 1870s. It was accelerated between 1885 and the end of the Witte era (1906), but only in the last decade before the First World War did an urbanized industrial proletariat really come into existence in Russia.

By the middle of the nineteenth century, however, other changes were beginning. Industry was gathering pace, and certain sections of the population were beginning to enjoy more modern conditions. But the peasants still stood out as the great exception. In practice, if not in law, their position was scarcely better than that of the slaves in the southern United States. They suffered from a threefold bondage: first, to their lord; secondly, to the *mir*; and thirdly, to their family group. While the third of these forms of bondage came to be ignored, the second was considered sacrosanct. In the reign of Nicholas I even liberals such as Alexander Herzen regarded the *mir*, or village community, as an untouchable national institution, the manifestation of a community principle common to all Slavs from time immemorial. They saw in it the real owner of the land, an organization which shouldered responsibility for all its members and which therefore, they thought, preserved Russia from the social problems that haunted western Europe. It was a fantastic theory; but right down to 1906, it prevented the abrogation of the outdated and harmful *mir* organization.

Bound by this system, which so many well-intentioned people erroneously supported, the peasants lived in almost unmitigated misery. Their distress manifested itself in the revolts, large and small, which broke out again and again during the whole Petersburg period. The idea of emancipating them into a more humane existence was encouraged both by humanitarian motives and by the demand for unrestricted wage-earning labour, but until 1855 was not put into practice. Few landowners wished to abandon the old system, and as they were the strongest element in the state—stronger even than the Tsar—their view prevailed. The privileged nobility ruled the state indirectly through the officers' corps, which was also for the most part made up of nobles, and since the government was dependent on their co-operation and support, it could not prevent them from exploiting the peasants. Occasionally, as in the *Family Chronicle* of the elder Aksakov (1791–1859), the relations between landowners and peasants are portrayed in idyllic, patriarchal terms; but such accounts, whatever their literary merits, misrepresent the woeful reality.

113 *A Monastic Refectory* (1865–75), by Perov, satirizes the corruption of monasteries. Suppliants are ignored while a grand local lady is attended to

Compared with the peasantry the urban population was still numerically a negligible quantity. It consisted largely of petty tradesmen, with a thin layer of industrialists beginning to emerge, and it would be an exaggeration to speak of it as a 'middle class'. There were also the intelligentsia, the men of letters who, while part and parcel of society, already felt themselves to be outside the class structure. Since the time of Alexander I they had been the representatives of a growing social and intellectual opposition.

Such, broadly speaking, was the disjointed and discordant social structure that existed in Russia in the time of Nicholas I, dominated by the absolutism of the imperial autocracy. In principle this was unlimited, but it did not, in fact, extend to control of the administration. In appearance a military despotism, this autocracy depended on the support of the decaying nobility, the army, and the bureaucracy, which in recompense were allowed to hold full sway. The working people had no say in government at all; they were merely instruments. Nor was the situation improved by the conquests of Peter the Great and Catherine II, of Alexander I and Nicholas I. Their effect was to intensify the centralization of government. Through the annexation of the Baltic provinces, of Poland, Lithuania, Finland and Bessarabia, Russia had acquired a large number of non-Russian subjects and had become a composite state. But it was ruled from St Petersburg in a more centralized way than ever before, and the government adopted a policy of unification and 'Russification' as an answer to the discontent of the subject peoples. It was determined to establish internal unity, if necessary by force, to impose the Russian language and the Orthodox faith. Thus the reign of Nicholas I saw the beginnings of Great Russian nationalism and of a policy which was bound in the end to lead to difficulties.

The government also continued its efforts towards territorial expansion, which it treated as though it were its *raison d'être*. After 1813 no one threatened Russia, but the government pressed on ever further, towards the sea and ice-free harbours, at the same time beginning that 'pursuit of the frontier' which provided the impetus for colonization across the Urals as well as in the Caucasus. It was no longer a question of defence. The empire had expanded far beyond its national limits. Where would its lust for territory now drive it: to the Straits, to Constantinople, or to dominion over the Balkans?

Inevitably Russia's expansionist tendencies affected its relations with the rest of Europe. Westernization, followed by territorial acquisitions on that frontier, had brought Russia far more closely into contact with western Europe. In its political and economic structure it followed European models and it aspired to do so in the cultural field. But its policy of rigorously isolating itself from the West meant that for most Europeans the conditions prevailing in Russia were as enigmatic as the sphinx. Though Russia was now a member—indeed, the dominating member—of the European consortium, its ambitions in the Near East made it a permanent source of international unrest and a threat to European peace. It was always prepared to take up arms against liberal movements in western Europe, and for this reason was feared and hated.

This aggressive foreign policy undoubtedly overtaxed Russia's strength, a fact which became apparent to all under Nicholas I. The government and the people had been at loggerheads for centuries; now there was added a conflict between the state and society, or at least between the state and the intelligentsia. In the first half of the nineteenth century a powerful and resourceful intellectual and political opposition arose, which became an important factor in the period of reform inaugurated by the Crimean War.

The opposition was led largely by men of letters, and for this reason some indication of the part they played in Russian history is necessary. Our starting-point is Mikhail Vassilyevich Lomonosov (1711–65), whose intellectual achievements, especially his use of language, matched Peter the Great's in the political sphere. Through Lomonosov the Russian language became a wonderfully pliable and expressive literary vehicle. After his death a period of astonishingly rapid development began, which soon secured Russian writing a place in world literature. Its special characteristics were evident at an early stage—sympathy with the people, a craving for social justice and liberty, hostility to oppression of all kinds. It was, in short, a literature of criticism and opposition. For decades it was the mouthpiece of Russian opinion, in a way that had no parallel in any other country. The ideas it expressed could not be openly proclaimed because of the censorship, but they were introduced indirectly into literature and philosophy, where a great deal could be implied. Literary works passed quickly from hand to hand and were greedily devoured; criticism, if only hinted at, was understood and people learnt to read between the lines. In this way, Russian literature performed an immense service for over a century, helping to form the views of individuals, to express collective desires, and to shape parties. It was for the most part functional, i.e. tendentious socio-political literature, and very rarely pure art; its study is indispensable for an understanding of Russia during the Petersburg period.

After Lomonosov and the writers of Catherine II's time the proselytizing liberalism of letters became more widely felt. This was evident in the case of the Decembrists. It also drew new inspiration from contemporary philosophy, notably the German philosophy of Schelling and Hegel, which exerted immense influence in the Russian intellectual world. Another influence was Romanticism; but Romanticism in Russia soon acquired that realistic trait which preoccupation with the people introduced into Russian writing. It threw up a poet of world renown, Alexander Sergeyevich Pushkin (1799–1837). Though Pushkin died at an early age and was unable to complete his work, he was one of the greatest of Russian poets, a master of language and metre. In *Eugène Onegin* he drew the first unforgettable portrait of the 'superfluous man', a figure who reappears in Russian literature in different guises down to the time of Chekhov, and who embodies the tragedy, weakness and instability of the intellectual in the confined and oppressive atmosphere of Russia.

The literary trends, the philosophical speculation and the currents of historical thought prevalent in the 1840s led to the two great intellectual movements which divided and dominated Russian parties and programmes, right down to 1914. These were the Westernizers and the Slavophiles. Both were obsessed with the problem of Russia's place in history. The Westernizers argued that Russia could only fulfil its task in association with western Europe and by following the Western path. They believed in European civilization of which they held Russia to be a part, and they admired Peter the Great

114, 115, 116 Lomonosov, the grammarian of the Enlightenment, Pushkin, Russia's greatest poet, and Gogol, her first major novelist

because he had linked Russia to the West. In practice this led them to formulate reform programmes and advocate popular representation, according to Western models. The Slavophiles, on the other hand, based their views on the distinctive character of the Russian race, which in their opinion occupied a special position, apart from Europe and, indeed, hostile to it. It was this special position, the product of history and the Russian 'national spirit', which accounted for the 'mission' Russia was destined to fulfil in the world. Its foundations, they believed, were Orthodoxy and the community principle embodied in the *mir*.

The conflict between Westernizers and Slavophiles gave rise to many other trends and groupings in nineteenth-century Russia. It also revealed the country's uncertainty about its ultimate purpose. This was hotly debated, and on the whole the dispute had a vitalizing influence; but it also deepened the rift and increased the confusion amongst the intellectuals. Both parties, however, were always in agreement on one thing—the inadequacy of the existing state. Without these two movements, the development towards liberalism, nihilism and socialism which followed would be quite unintelligible. Alexander Herzen, Bakunin and many other leading intellectuals occupied a place in their ranks; outstanding in the realm of literature was the satirist Nikolai Vassilyevich Gogol (1809–52). Meanwhile Turgenev, Dostoyevsky and Tolstoy were growing to maturity.

137

The Church played no part in this great intellectual activity, which flourished in spite of censorship and police interference. On the other hand, the Establishment showed considerable skill in using the Church, which was part of the trinity of Autocracy, Orthodoxy and Nationalism on which the state rested, for its own ends. Nicholas I exploited Orthodoxy in a way secular-minded rulers like Peter the Great and Catherine II had never done, with far-reaching consequences for the development of nationalism and Russification.

The intellectual movements of the period down to 1855, then, were characterized by a critical attitude towards the existing state and a demand for reform. Their strength was underestimated by the Tsar and his government at the time, and even today their fertile germinal quality is not always fully appreciated. The men behind these movements were responsible for the dawn of a new age in Russia. They were bent on reform, and often prepared to use force for this purpose. After the demoralization brought about by the defeats during the Crimean War, their criticism could no longer be disregarded. The government itself was forced to introduce reforms. In the realm of ideas the intellectual movements we have described had prepared the way for reform by awakening both the social conscience and the national consciousness. All now depended on whether the government would pay sufficient heed. If it did not— if the Tsar and the ruling classes failed to see the writing on the wall— there was little doubt that the ferment started by these movements would spread into revolutionary channels.

THE AGE OF ALEXANDER II (1855–81)

Alexander II succeeded to a bankrupt régime. Personally, he may be considered the most attractive figure in the Romanov dynasty. Son of a Prussian princess, he had in him more Hohenzollern than Romanov traits, and found it hard to adopt the Russian way of life. He always felt closely attached to the Prussian army and the Prussian royal family. He was by nature soft and tractable, unlike his rigid father, but even so he was no weakling. Despite his pliancy, he had the ability to resist external influences. He had received a remarkably good upbringing. From his tutor, the poet V. A. Zhukovsky

117 Alexander II
takes the winter air
in his *droshky*, 1881

(1783–1852), he learned to appreciate the importance of his humanitarian duties, and this teaching corresponded to his own natural in-
clinations and to his actual plans. Ruthlessness, cruelty and wilfulness were alien to his nature. He was a good man, and in the first
half of his reign at least his good intentions were realized.

On his accession to the throne it was clear to him that the state,
tottering and exhausted as it was, would need thorough overhaul and
reform if he and the dynasty were to survive. So far as an autocratic
Tsar could, he kept an open mind regarding the reforming movements discussed in the last chapter. But he wanted reform to be
initiated from the traditional seat of authority, to come from above
and be offered to the people as a gift.

Realizing that the first necessity was to end the war, which was as
good as lost, he decided to accept the consequences of military defeat.
In September 1855 Sevastopol fell. Since the Western powers did not
follow up this success and Austria did not attack, there was no

pressing need to end hostilities, but Russia's total exhaustion precluded all possibility of further fighting. Hence Alexander concluded the Peace of Paris on 30 March 1856. The regions south of the Danube which Russia had acquired earlier were given up. The Black Sea was neutralized. Russia was not permitted to maintain a fleet there nor to erect fortifications. The Straits were closed to warships of all nations. Russia had to surrender the protectorate it claimed over the Balkan Christians, who were now placed under the protection of all the great powers. So far as the Near East and the Balkans were concerned, Russia's activities were severely circumscribed. At the same time, it lost its dominating position in Europe, and France under Napoleon III took the leading rôle. In all these ways the Crimean War marked a turning-point both in European and in Russian history.

The ending of the Crimean War cleared the way for the Age of Reform. The reforms carried out under Alexander made a far deeper impression on Russia than did the process of Westernization under Peter the Great and Catherine II. If they had introduced new technological methods and stirred up the intellectual atmosphere, the Age of Reform struck at the very heart of the established order. It altered the whole social structure and re-shaped the political system on Western lines. Both Alexander himself and the more intelligent of his advisers were aware of the possibility of revolution. True, the Tsar may not have been sufficiently far-sighted to recognize the full implications of his changes; he did not perceive that a new era was beginning which would complete the transition of Russia from medieval collectivism to modern individualism. But he was wise enough to declare that 'It is better to abolish serfdom from above, than to await the time when it will bring itself to an end from beneath'. Not many rulers in a comparable position have shown such insight. In this respect Alexander II's achievement is greater than that of Peter the Great or Catherine II. He set out to combat the threat of revolution by reforms which he himself initiated.

Before we turn to his reforms, let us glance briefly at the forces of liberalism in Alexander's day, as they had crystallized out of the social and intellectual ferment of the first half of the nineteenth century. Considering its fear of revolution, it is not suprising that the government mistrusted these forces. They were still prevented from openly expressing their views, but after 1855 they were allowed to develop somewhat more freely. This could be seen in journalism, in literature and in the first stirrings of political parties. On the other hand, it is striking how quickly the liberal movement became radical, with the result that the government, which was in fact quite prepared to undertake reforms, dissociated itself from the reformers. The old rift, in other words, could not so easily be bridged. And understanding was further hampered by the impact of materialist philosophy and revolutionary ideologies from the West.

These were the circumstances in which a widespread radical and revolutionary opposition came to a head, of which N. G. Chernyshevsky (1828–89), a man of radical and vaguely socialist views, was the leader. Associated with him were Dobrolyubov (1836–81) and Pisarev (1840–1908), who, like Chernyshevsky, were persecuted by the government and honoured as martyrs by their supporters.

118, 119 Chernyshevsky and Dobrolyubov, early champions of the radical free Press in the periodical *Sovremennik* ('Contemporary')

120, 121 Bakunin (*left*) and Herzen (*above*)
Nihilist and revolutionary writers

From abroad the great *émigré*, Alexander Herzen (1812–70), provided inspiration and a driving force. Intellectually he towered above the rest. Between 1857 and 1863 his periodical *Kolokol*, or *The Bell*, though proscribed in Russia, was read by everyone and exercised a profound influence. Every social issue was hotly debated: the family, marriage, taxation, the status of women, the emancipation of the peasants, representation of the people. At the same time every possible variety of Western socialism made its impact—Saint-Simon, Proudhon, Fourier and Bakunin were all avidly read and digested—and with it went an indigenous revolutionary socialism of purely Russian origin. It was a 'raging sea', as the title of a novel of the period characteristically expressed it, and out of it arose the phenomenon known as Nihilism, which people at the time regarded as the most serious of all forms of revolutionary infection. The Nihilist was not, as is often thought, identical with the terrorist or assassin of a later period. The latter had some sort of faith, for which he was prepared to risk his life; for the former there was only nothingness. He was the completely rootless individual, who denied the whole existing order and wished to be free from all social and moral bonds, who rejected his relationship with society and claimed to live in complete independence as an individual. Turgenev (1818–83) was the first to portray this type in his novel *Fathers and Sons*. Dostoyevsky's character, Stavrogin, was an even more extreme

КОЛОКОЛЪ

ПРИБАВОЧНЫЕ ЛИСТЫ КЪ ПОЛЯРНОЙ ЗВѢЗДѢ

VIVOS VOCO!

(ВТОРОЕ ИЗДАНІЕ)

ЛИСТЪ 1.

1 Іюля 1857.

123 The medal of 1863 (*above*) [mar]ked the first decade of a free Russian [pre]ss in London. The bell (*Kolokol*) repre[sent]s the publication with which Herzen [hop]ed to 'rouse the sleeping soul of [Rus]sia' (*right*)

124, 125 The novelists Dostoyevsky (*left*) and Turgenev (*above*) wrote profoundly of revolutionary movements

example. But Nihilism, though for the authorities the most extreme revolutionary creed, was confined to a limited, often half-educated section of the intelligentsia. The peasants, the rising *bourgeoisie*, the property owners and the larger part of the civil service were not involved in the cultural crisis, which mainly affected students, a few young officials and officers, and dissatisfied members of the urban proletariat which was just beginning to emerge.

This tangle of interlocked movements is portrayed in masterly fashion by Turgenev's social novels. Though his work was politically motivated, he was always a creative and truly European writer. The miserable conditions of the peasants are poignantly described in *A Sportsman's Sketches*. Then there was I. A. Goncharov (1812–91), whose novel *Oblomov* portrays the true Russian in contrast to the Westernized Russian of German extraction. N. A. Nekrassov (1821–78), author of the poem *Who Can Be Happy and Free in Russia?*, should also be mentioned here, whilst the great Dostoyevsky was already coming into prominence with *The House of the Dead* (1861) and his novel *Crime and Punishment* (1866).

It is not surprising that the violent intellectual ferment frightened the authorities. However divided otherwise, the intelligentsia was united in its opposition to the state. It was developing an extreme radicalism which, though not yet organized into parties or programmes, was inspired by a vague kind of socialism, and against which the government and its conservative associates were unable to produce any convincing ideological weapons.

This was the situation in which, around 1858, Alexander II began his work of reform. Its most important aspect, the basis of all further reform, was the emancipation of the peasants. Enthusiastically received at first, it soon encountered opposition from the landowners, but was nevertheless carried through. Its practical implementation was the work of a group of enlightened, humane and discerning officials with Nikolay Milyutin at their head. They deserve the utmost praise. They were aided by liberal circles at court, under the leadership of the Grand Duchess Helena Pavlovna, but their work was rendered increasingly difficult by the machinations of reactionary landowners, whom the Tsar was too weak to oppose energetically.

The reform had two aspects, the one concerned with the personal freedom of the peasants, the other with their lands. On the former, agreement was quickly reached. By a decree of 3 March 1861, serfdom was abolished. No compensation had to be paid for their actual freedom, but a long, hard struggle took place over the peasant's land. Should the emancipated peasant have land, or not? This was the central problem. Most landowners were in favour of the latter. The landless peasants would then have been at their disposal, an amorphous mass of wage-earning labourers whom they could use as they saw fit. The more reasonable landowners, and those who desired emancipation for humanitarian reasons, opposed this plan. In their view it was madness, for by creating a landless proletariat, it would establish the basis for agrarian revolution on a vast scale. Finally, the party which favoured the retention of land by the emancipated peasants carried the day. But there was no agreement about the conditions. After lengthy negotiations it was finally agreed that the serfs' lands were the property of the landowners, who should be compensated, although, in fact, the lands had been farmed by the peasants for centuries. The peasants, needless to say, had no voice in the negotiations.

Once the decision was reached, the number of acres of arable land the peasants should be allowed in each region was established by a complicated method. An estimate was made of the capital value of their dues and services, and on this basis it was determined how much each peasant should pay. As might be expected, the peasants received less land than they needed for subsistence and had to pay more than its value. The consequence was widespread land-hunger. Individual agreements were to have been freely negotiated between landowners and peasants within the terms of the settlement. In fact, the state intervened straight away, paying the compensation due from the peasants to the landowners, with the result that the latter received ready cash and the possibility of employing hired labour from the very beginning. The peasants, on the other hand, were in debt to the state, to which they were supposed to pay back their loans over a period of forty-nine years. This was the so-called 'redemption money' which rapidly became a millstone around the peasants' necks and was to cause a great deal of trouble in the future; though finally, when it became evident that the payments were too great a burden, they were remitted.

These were the main terms of the Edict of Emancipation. It freed 47 million people. Peasants on the crown lands had received their freedom somewhat earlier, on slightly better terms; the additional number involved here was 22 million. The effect of the whole vast operation was to transform the existing social order, to bring about radical changes in agriculture, and to open a new era of wage-earning labour and capitalism. 'Man of Galilee, you have won,' cried Herzen, acknowledging the Tsar's achievement.

But our praise for Alexander II's initiative in freeing the serfs needs qualifying in a number of respects. First, the Tsar was to some extent responsible for the measure's limited effectiveness. The inadequacy of the plots of land allotted to the peasants and the heavy burden of the redemption-payments led directly to the agrarian crisis which was plainly evident by the 'seventies. Secondly, nothing was done about the *mir*, or peasant community, which continued in existence until 1906. Its weaknesses were simply not recognized. No one would admit that its organization was out of date and that it hampered and frustrated the peasants. It was unable to help its members. As the population increased and the land was split into small parcels, the *mir* was unable to provide land for them all, or to prevent the emergence of a landless proletariat. In fact, it was an antiquated institution which should have been replaced either by a system of private peasant ownership or by a form of co-operative. Preserved largely for sentimental reasons, it became a source of evils and anomalies which also contributed to the growing agrarian crisis.

No large-scale peasant movement occurred for a number of years as a result of these conditions though already in 1861–2 more than 2,000 cases of local peasant unrest were reported. But it was not long before the peasant communities, which were supposed to be self-administering units under the control of the rural districts (*volost*), fell into decay. This was partly the result of sheer poverty, partly the consequence of social differentiation. Within the villages there appeared an upper stratum of rich peasants, or *kulaks*, and a lower, poverty-stricken stratum, the village proletarians and semi-proletarians. These landless or nearly landless peasants were to be the mainstay of the agrarian revolution.

The emancipation of the peasants was by far the most important of Alexander II's reforms, but by no means the only one. A whole series of other measures followed. The *Decree concerning Rural Authorities in the Gouvernements and Districts* (1864) established local self-government of a limited sort, the local assembly (*zemstvo*) being reinforced by representatives of the nobility, the towns and the peasants. In 1870 there was a new ordinance for the cities. In 1884 the law courts were brought into line with modern European legal practice, a measure which was probably the best of all Alexander's reforms. Modification of the censorship followed in 1865 though it was still far from satisfactory. In 1871, regulations were issued for the reform of secondary schools, followed by others for elementary schools. Though the latter measures already showed the influence of reactionary trends, it was to be applauded that state, *zemstvo* and Church all now began to tackle the desperately neglected problem of elementary education. Another reform abolished the hereditary clerical caste and brought the clergy into line with the new social structure. A budget was introduced, but there was no comprehensive reform of the system of taxation as a whole. Finally, there was Alexander's introduction of general conscription in 1874, on which the armed forces were based until the end of the First World War.

Thus his reforming activity covered practically every aspect of national life. Taken as a whole, it was of fundamental importance. It might have heralded the opening of a new age in Russia if, in the second half of his reign, reactionary tendencies had not got the upper hand. From then until 1905 there was a return to a rigid conservative absolutism which was hostile to all reform.

It might reasonably have been expected that the work of reform would be completed by some form of popular representation. This was demanded by both the radical and the moderate reformers, but it was refused by the Tsar and by the ruling factions. Despite the concessions which had been wrung from them, the Tsar himself, the aristocracy and the bureaucracy were determined to maintain their position, and in this they were successful. From the middle of the 'sixties, reaction was once again in the saddle. The reforms could not, of course, be undone; Russia, after 1865, was and remained completely different from the Russia of Nicholas I. But their effects were greatly weakened, and the hope of further harmonious development was dashed.

The reaction which set in after about 1865 brought about a critical situation which was aggravated by the effects of Russian foreign policy. Alexander II was no advocate of aggression and expansion. He wanted peace, and indeed he kept it for a considerable period. It was not his fault that in 1863 he had to deal with a new uprising in Poland, where he desired to introduce a liberal régime, or that the intervention of England, France and Austria raised the threat of a great European war. Since Prussia stood fast on Russia's side, the crisis was overcome. But it led to an intensification of Russian nationalism. It mouthpiece was Mikhail Katkov (1818–87), now rapidly becoming the chief spokesman of public opinion, and as this nationalism grew stronger it led to a policy of Russification, especially in Poland, the western territories and the Baltic provinces.

Under Alexander II, territorial expansion greatly increased Russia's power in Asia, and from the beginning of the 'seventies there was increasing tension with England. The two countries, however, avoided coming to blows. Russia's colonial possessions in Asia were rounded off without war, and they became the most tightly knit colonial empire in the world. The fusion of this empire into a unity—a unity upon which the Soviet Union's position in Asia rests today—was one of the most remarkable achievements in history, with which only the development of the Roman and the British Empires can compare. Not that Alexander II was personally responsible for this; it was brought about, rather, by the impetus of commercial and industrial capitalism, which, freed from the old restrictions, began to press for markets, new sources of raw materials and a field from which other powers were excluded.

There were two main phases of Russian expansion in Asia. The one saw the completion of the conquest and pacification of the

Caucasus, from the Black Sea (1859) to the Caspian (1864); the other was marked by the Far Eastern treaties (1858 and 1860), by which Russia acquired the regions of the Amur and Ussuri. In this way it absorbed the whole of Siberia and reached the Pacific Ocean, becoming in the process China's neighbour and a Far Eastern power. In central Asia it pushed forward to Tashkent (1865), Samarkand (1868), Bokhara (1868), Khiva (1873) and Kokand (1876). This great surge of expansion seemed to Europeans to express an elemental urge which might equally well turn against the West. The forces behind it were never clearly understood, even in Russia itself, but they included the lust for power, the need for new markets and sources of supply, the desire to reach the sea and its harbours, and above all the pursuit of the open frontier across the unending steppes and desert, the inherent striving of a colonial people—which the Great Russians were and still are—unable to establish colonies overseas and therefore compelled to press on inexorably over land.

It was, in any case, a movement of world-wide importance. It meant the extension of European influence in Asia, the opening-up of areas hitherto outside the main current of history, and the fulfilment of a civilizing mission, which the Russians certainly believed they were performing in Asia. In the context of international politics, on the other hand, it increased the danger of a clash. It meant, in particular, that Russia and England were brought into close contact in Asia, resulting in a rivalry which was for decades one of the focal points of international tension. In Afghanistan and Persia, in India and the Far East, there was growing friction between the two great powers during Alexander's reign. Furthermore, the position Russia had acquired in the Caucasus allowed it to re-open the 'Eastern question'.

In spite of its expansion in central Asia and the Far East, the 'Eastern question' was still Russia's main concern. This became apparent in the late 'seventies. Alexander II himself had no wish to re-open it; all he desired was to maintain the 'League of the three Emperors' with Germany and Austria established in 1872. But the growth of nationalism and pan-Slavism drove him against his will into a new conflict with Turkey (April 1877). In January 1878, Russian troops advanced across the Balkans and laid siege to Adrianople. Russian forces had never before penetrated so far. Constantinople and the Dardanelles lay close at hand. The Peace of San Stefano (3 March 1878) saw the Russians dictating their own terms. But at this point England and Austria intervened with a threat of war, and Russia, exhausted and distracted by troubles at home, was forced to give way. The settlement reached at the Congress of Berlin (13 June–13 July 1878) largely reflected English and Austrian demands. For Russia the outcome of its military victories was a bitter political defeat, the blame for which was laid on Germany. It was felt that Germany should have given more support, which Bismarck was not prepared to do. Actually Russia lost nothing tangible through the events of 1877 and 1878. What mattered was the addition of a new enmity with England to the old enmity with Austria. No less important was the cooling of relations with Germany. This was hastened by Bismarck who, with unnecessary speed and little justification, concluded an alliance with Austria in 1879, by which he involved the German Empire, which at that time had no real interests in the Near East, in Austro-Russian rivalries. Thus he sowed the seeds of future war between Germany and Russia.

Driven this way and that in foreign policy, a pacifist at heart but expansionist in practice, Alexander II had also to struggle with an internal situation which was becoming more and more critical. To this his own reactionary tendencies, the failure to follow through his early reforms, the increasing power of the opposition, and the exhaustion brought about by war, all contributed. On the one hand, aggressive nationalism drove him into a dangerous war; on the other, the opposition was to become increasingly radical, revolutionary and terroristic. For the time being, the peaceful populist movement—the so-called *narodnichestvo*, inspired by Herzen and Bakunin —was in the ascendant. Young intellectuals were called upon to 'go to the people', to bridge the gap between the educated classes and the peasants, to overcome the old social cleavages not by revolutionary activity but by constructive, educative work in the village communities. It was a movement which sought to build on the foundation of a native socialism, and there was a great deal of

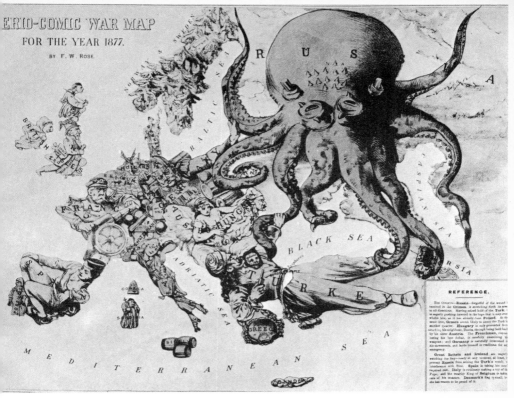

126 Britain's fear that the Russian military monster would swallow up the whole of Europe is expressed in this 'serio-comic' map of the time of the Russo-Turkish War, 1877

genuine devotion to the people in the ideology of the *narodniki*. But it proved a failure. The peasants declined the help of these voluntary teachers and helpers, whom they regarded as 'little lords', and the government thought their activities were hostile to the state and effected a number of arrests followed by heavy sentences.

This failure provided the incentive for another party which wanted revolution, and sought to bring it about by assassination and terror. This movement, *Zemlya i Volya* or 'Land and Freedom', derived its inspiration from Bakunin and Nechayev, and sought to bring about revolution by propaganda, as Chernyshevsky had advocated. It regarded assassination as one form of this propaganda. Something of the Marxist idea of a conspiratorial party of militant

151

127, 128 Repin's sketch of 1879 (*above*) shows the arrest of a propagandist. *Below*, the Nihilists implicated in the assassination of the Tsar receive on the scaffold the comforts of the Church they had foresworn

129 Plekhanov, the writer,
reacted against
individualist anarchy
by becoming a Marxist

workers was present in it, but as yet conditions were not ripe for
such a development. There seemed to be no alternative to pure
terrorism, and the 'administrative section' was created to organize
it. But at the conventions in Lipets and Voronezh in the summer
of 1879, the revolutionaries split into two groups, the Black
Partition (*Cherny Peredel*) with a programme of somewhat ill-
defined agrarian socialism, and the People's Will (*Narodnaya Volya*)
which, convinced of the impossibility of a mass uprising, relied
entirely on the elimination of leading personalities by assassination;
this, it believed, would bring about the collapse of the hated régime.
In the end, its activities were directed exclusively against the Tsar
on whom the executive committee of the *Narodnaya Volya* passed
sentence of death. These tactics were rejected by Russian Marxists,
for the attitude of the group was unrealistic and had little to do with
socialism. But one assassination followed another; and the con-
spirators caused considerable unrest and insecurity.

The last decade of Alexander II's reign saw Marxism make its first
inroads into Russia. The Marxist writer Plekhanov (1857–1918)
began his literary activity at this time. A more important factor

153

130, 131 Loris-Melikov (*below*) suppressed
revolutionary movements while trying to reconcile
the population with the government. *Russian
Civilisation*, a cartoon of 1880 (*right*)—the year before
Alexander's assassination—attacks the Imperial bear's
policy 'as approved by W. G. [Gladstone] & Co.'

was the development of an urban industrial proletariat which came
into existence as a result of the emancipation of the peasants and the
growth of capitalism. Such a class had not previously existed in
Russia. Its rise made possible the establishment of a conscious
workers' movement, the first beginning of which can be traced to the
years 1865–70. In 1865 there were 1,425 factories in Russia with
392,718 workers and a turnover of 296 million roubles. By 1880 the
number had increased to 16,564 factories with 616, 925 workers and
a turnover of 731 million roubles. The old factory system based on
serfs had been replaced by a modern, capitalist organization with
free enterprise and wage-earning labour. This new capitalism made
possible the development of the railway system and of banking, and
facilitated the emergence of a real middle class and a modern working
class. Though Russia's industry still lagged behind that of western

Europe, its economy entered a new phase. If Alexander II did not attain the same level of personal greatness as Peter I and Catherine II, the years covered by his reign had more profound effects than theirs on the course of his country's development.

In the midst of these changes, and the unrest arising from the revolutionary movement, Alexander II once again made a genuine attempt at reform. He found in Count Loris-Melikov an energetic adviser who was given extraordinary powers as a kind of Minister of Reform. On 13 March 1881, Alexander signed a decree which, though it did not grant a constitution, seemed to point the way to a constitutional system by associating elected representatives with the business of legislation. On the same day he was assassinated. In spite of the existing tension, the assassination did not lead to revolution. The political and social order stood firm.

Alexander III (1881–94), a clumsy, ungifted, obstinate man, took over the government on his father's death without the slightest difficulty. He was determined not to follow the path Alexander II had latterly embarked on. He intended rather to return to the rigorous absolutism of Nicholas I, and to maintain it by a reactionary policy based on police rule. His programme consisted of the famous trinity of Autocracy, Orthodoxy and Nationalism; he wanted to rule as an absolute monarch, which, considering the size of his Empire, was a total impossibility. He always claimed that his outlook was profoundly Russian; in fact, he remained pre-occupied with irrelevant details. His policy of Russification made him the sponsor of a nationalism which grew increasingly aggressive. Without the slightest trace of greatness, or even of the majesty Nicholas I had possessed, he followed in the latter's footsteps; he was a foolish, narrow-minded man who lacked self-reliance and was entirely dependent on his teacher Pobedonostsev (1827–1907).

The latter, though in fact no more than chief procurator of the Holy Synod (1880–1907), controlled the internal politics of Russia under Alexander III and also for many years under Nicholas II. Only finance and economic and foreign affairs were free from his interference. A gifted and well-educated lawyer, with strong theological leanings, Pobedonostsev combined the intellectual training of the nineteenth century with the scholasticism of the thirteenth. Dostoyevsky is said to have based the character of the Grand Inquisitor in his novel *The Brothers Karamazov* on this remarkable man, an anachronism even for Russia, who was for a quarter of a century the effective ruler of the empire, and its evil spirit. If any individual was personally responsible for the Revolution it was he.

It is a remarkable fact that, apart from local peasant unrest, there was no popular rising against the oppressive régime between 1881 and 1905. It seemed as though the people were sunk in apathy. They allowed themselves to be oppressed and exploited, with the result that the impression gained ground, particularly in Germany, that they were a weak, docile race, incapable of rebellion or resistance.

132, 133 Alexander III (*left*) turned for advice to his old tutor Konstantin Pobedonostsev, a man who wrote, 'What is this freedom by which so many minds are agitated . . . which leads the people so often to misfortune?'

Neither the unrest among the peasants, nor the increasing numbers of strikes among the industrial workers were sufficient to counteract the impression of a state pining away passively under an unassailable autocrat. But the outside world exaggerated the power of the Russian government, just as it had done in the time of Nicholas I. For in the deathly silence an underground network was in operation. Its weapon was no longer terrorism, though assassination continued, but rather the organization of a mass movement among the industrial proletariat in the towns. The first Social Democratic organization came into existence in 1883. The Marxists worked systematically to organize and educate, and prepare the ground for revolution. Unrest continued among the students and younger intellectuals, and in 1902 their participation in the movement was warmly endorsed by the workers. Thus, two distinct revolutionary elements were emerging, which the state could only oppose with brutal and ultimately ineffective police measures.

134, 135, 136 The oppressiveness of an inadequately liberalized régime. *Above left*, a woman under twenty years' sentence at Ust-Kara Prison in Siberia. *Above right*, convicts chained

In his accession manifesto, proclaiming his faith in 'the power and rights of autocracy', Alexander III adopted a reactionary policy which revived the old system of government, and determined the course of Russian history for the next twenty-five years. No one can say whether the policies adopted at the end of Alexander II's reign would have led to peaceful reform, but there is no doubt that those chosen in turn by his son and grandson led to revolution. For Nicholas II (1894–1917) continued along the same reactionary road as Alexander III; his accession brought no essential change. Compared with his father he was a weakling who simply allowed the existing system to continue, and his reign was as devoid of positive results as Alexander III's. It is true that neither of them abrogated Alexander II's reforms, but they rendered them ineffective with the aid of the bureaucracy and the police. The policy of Russification they pursued in Poland and the Baltic provinces, and later in Finland and elsewhere in the Empire, was imposed by force and can hardly be regarded as constructive. Nor was there anything positive in their financial policy, which only increased the burden on the people and so heightened the tension.

to wheelbarrows for offences against prison discipline. *Below*, female convicts fetching water at Nershinsk Prison, 1898

It is true that the twenty-five years between 1881 and 1905 saw major economic developments; but these had nothing to do with the policies of the two rulers, who understood nothing about economics. The dominant factor was the agrarian crisis which now culminated in a series of disastrous famines. There had been serious misgivings about the agrarian situation and the way the emancipation of the peasants had been carried out ever since the 'seventies; but nothing was done about either. Then in 1890–91, European Russia was confronted by full-scale famine. The suffering attracted enormous attention both at home and abroad, but it was not an isolated event. Between 1891 and 1914 there were no less than twelve bad harvests. The exhaustion of the soil and the overburdening of the peasants were such that in the great granary of Europe—even in the Black Earth fertile region—starvation was chronic. Moreover, the situation was aggravated by the government's agrarian policy. Russia's heavy foreign loans, the pursuit of its expansionist foreign policy, encouraged the export of grain not merely for the benefit of the nobility and the capitalist classes, but also in the interests of the state, which needed foreign exchange to pay its foreign creditors. And the peasant, scarcely able to live on the yield of his harvest, was forced to pay even higher taxes. This was the vicious circle in which three-quarters of the Tsar's subjects were caught up. It was also a very shaky foundation for the new capitalist system which was rapidly taking shape. Russia had been propelled into capitalism by Alexander II's reforms, and at the time it was believed that the capitalist phase would be superseded and its accompanying social problems solved through the peasant community.

In reality, capitalism followed the same course and had the same consequences in Russia as in western Europe. The advent of railways, loans raised abroad for railway building, the impact of foreign investment which the government encouraged, the growth of heavy industry and the accumulation of industrial capital, all contributed to this end. In 1877 the gross national product was valued at 541 million roubles, in 1897 at 1,816 million roubles. In the last twenty years of the nineteenth century, Russian industrial output quadrupled. The obverse of this seeming prosperity took the form of depressions,

137 During the famine of 1891–92, the peasants were reduced to stripping thatch from their houses to feed their livestock

strikes, wage disputes and a totally inadequate social policy. And the outcome was the growing class-consciousness of the industrial proletariat. In the heart of old Russia the textile industry was transformed by mechanization. Then it was the turn of the iron industry, stimulated by large government orders. The changes were most clearly visible in St Petersburg and in frontier-towns like Riga and Reval. At the same time, Polish industry grew up around Warsaw and Lodz and entered into competition with the old Russian centres. To judge by the Tsar's reactionary policies, Russia seemed to be sinking into dull, rigid inertia; but in reality new forces were welling up within it, the forces of an imperialism which was increasingly involved in the international credit system and which at the same time determined the direction of foreign trade. It was both a class policy and a national policy, and it aimed simultaneously at self-sufficiency, and at economic and colonial expansion.

The implementation of this policy was placed in the hands of the Minister of Finance, who acquired a position of power without parallel in any other country. He was at one and the same time the representative of the new commercial and industrial classes and of the neo-mercantilist state. This great post was filled by Sergey Yulyevich Witte from 1893 to 1903. Witte was a man of undoubted ability. He has been criticized for what he left undone, but there is no doubt that through his efforts, capitalism in Russia advanced at breakneck speed. He applied the gold standard to the rouble in 1897, thus attracting investors. He created the state liquor monopoly as an important source of income, with the result that the drinking of spirits changed from a luxury to a daily habit, and the peasants and workers brought money into the coffers of the state by drinking away their wages. Witte drew on foreign, especially French, capital on a vast scale, so that Russia became one of the biggest debtor nations. He increased the export of grain and pursued a policy which favoured Russian industry by protecting the home market with tariffs, without disrupting foreign trade. This was the so-called 'Witte system'. Witte himself knew perfectly well that all this was based on shaky foundations, but he believed that the people could carry the burden until the economy was over the first hurdle. He hoped that industrialization would provide him with sufficient resources to carry through a vast programme of agrarian reorganization. This was probably a dangerous illusion from the beginning. But Witte was right in regarding peace as essential for the success of his policy. He was therefore opposed to the war with Japan which broke out in 1904. The war party forced him out of office, but after the interruption caused by the war (1904–5) and the revolution (1905–6) his successors continued, though less energetically, along the path he had outlined. They pushed ahead with industrialization and encouraged the growth of monopolies and finance. But there was still no machine industry, no motor-car industry and there were no large-scale chemical or metallurgical industries. Nor was there a fully developed banking system. In all these respects Russia lagged a generation behind western Europe, though it was following the same course. Westernization no longer meant that a few European artillery experts, merchants or writers came to Russia, but that European capital was linked with Russian capital and exerted an increasing influence over political relations, particularly with France, but later also with England.

138 Sergey Yulievich Witte, whose strong personality dominated Russian governments in the years before 1905. His efforts to create an industrial capitalist society in a few years were ruined by the Russo-Japanese War

Witte's successors after 1908 sought to increase the self-sufficiency of the Russian Empire. They attempted to integrate the different regions, for instance by creating an exchange of raw materials and products between the industrial sectors in European Russia west of the Urals and the colonial regions of the Caucasus, Turkestan and Siberia. To this end they extended the railway system. The construction of the trans-Siberian railway had been begun as early as 1889; it was now hastened. Railway links with Orenburg and Tashkent and with Tiflis were established, and lines to Teheran and even to the Persian Gulf were mooted. The idea was to ease the agrarian problem at home by settling Russian peasants in these far-off regions. The whole scheme was a gigantic piece of wishful imperialist thinking on the part of the generation before the First World War, stimulated by ardent nationalism. Even so, the entire economic, social and political structure was fundamentally altered by these developments.

In the first place, the position of the land-owning nobility was affected. Its members had been able to make their views prevail at the time of the emancipation of the peasants, but they derived no lasting advantages from it. They simply spent the capital received in compensation, and failed to adapt themselves to capitalist society. As early as the 'seventies their position was weakening, and despite the help they received from the state they never managed to regain a firm foothold. There were vast estates, especially in the south; 163

there were model estates; there were even profit-making estates; but in general, the agrarian crisis amongst the peasants was matched by a similar one amongst the nobility. Its clearest sign was the way they constantly disposed of their lands outside their class. This crisis brought no improvement in the agrarian situation or in the condition of the peasants, and undermined the class on which the absolute state was built.

The change in the nobility's economic position weakened their political influence. On the other hand, a substantial and clearly defined middle class had not yet emerged. Even by 1914 a *tiers état*, such as existed in France as early as 1789, and in Germany in the middle of the nineteenth century, was not evident in Russia. What middle-class elements there were, depended largely on the state. There may have been *bourgeois* pride, but there was no self-conscious, self-determining middle class.

All about these groups, both relatively small, and subject to them were the peasants who constituted the vast mass of the Russian population. According to the census of 1897 five-sixths of the population lived from agriculture and only one-sixth from industry. But by that time some ten million peasants were already proletarianized, i.e. they possessed no land and worked for wages. Although there were roughly ten million farms in Russia in 1903, Lenin calculated that no less than three and a half million of these belonged to peasants

who had not so much as a horse to their name, and so were unable to cultivate their land properly. There were about twenty million peasants with lesser holdings of land which were too small to live off, so that they had to look for supplementary paid work. In the villages the landless or almost landless peasants were under the domination of the *kulaks*, who were capitalist farmers and often usurers. There were about one and a half million *kulak* farms of this kind, and they comprised about half the total arable land.

The peasant masses were in a revolutionary mood, as at the time of Pugachev's revolt, but they lacked any unified purpose or organization. Hence, when defeat in the war with Japan created an internal crisis, it was the organized industrial proletariat that was best qualified to stir up revolution. Numerically, however, it was still weak. Even in 1914 there cannot have been more than three million industrial workers out of a total population of almost 170 millions. Moreover, the working class was not yet properly organized throughout the Empire, and therefore not fully effective. The working-class parties were still only small cells. But although Dostoyevsky, for instance, underestimated its importance, the working class played a significant rôle in the series of great strikes which began in the 1880s and continued until 1914. The general strike of October 1905, which resulted in the October Manifesto, was probably the world's first example of really effective political use of this weapon.

, 140 During the kes of 1905, an
llery battery
rols the streets
Moscow (*left*)
r suppressing
rioters. *Right*,
keters at the
tilov steel factory
St Petersburg,
ere workers were
d to attend *soviet*
etings

It was on these shifting foundations that Alexander III's state rested. Outwardly unchanged, it continued to operate with outmoded instruments and was ill-fitted to cope with the new social and economic conditions. The situation was not unlike that in France immediately before 1789, but the ruling powers refused to recognize the similarity. A few people, including Witte, were more clear-sighted, but they did not have sufficient power to bring about reforms. What held the 'Colossus with feet of clay' together in the first half of the period was Alexander III's peaceful foreign policy. He was the only member of the Romanov dynasty who did not fight a major war. He was hostile to Austria and England (because of the 'Eastern question' and Asia); there was tension with Germany, which not even Bismarck's policy (The 'League of the three Emperors', 1881 and 1884, and the Reinsurance Treaty of 1887) could allay; but with France he maintained a friendship which culminated in the alliance of 1894. In the Near East, Alexander III's policy was not essentially different from that of his predecessors, and nearly led to war in 1885 and 1886. But he did not want war, and was not himself a pan-Slavist. Nevertheless pan-Slavism, which aimed at the union of the Slav races, was a subversive and aggressive force in Russia. It was supported by the Army, by the Church and by certain publicists, and caused perpetual disquiet in Europe. But there was no agitation among the nobility or the middle classes as a whole in favour of the movement, and it never flourished among the Russian peasants and workers.

When Nicholas II succeeded to the throne, he inherited a position of great prestige in international politics. He intended, as his father had done, to preserve it in peace. He surprised the world with proposals for disarmament, and though they did not achieve their purpose, they did lead to the establishment of the permanent court of arbitration at the Hague. Shortly before, Nicholas had settled the disputes with Great Britain in central Asia by the so-called Pamir agreement of 1895, and those with Austria in the Balkans in 1897. But he was too weak to control the military and financial groups which had turned their attention to the Far East after the Sino-Japanese war of 1894 in order to secure ports, strategic bases and

141 Tsar Nicholas II,
Alexandra Fyodorovna
and Olga
with the Tsarina's
grandmother Victoria
and Edward,
Prince of Wales,
at Balmoral in 1896

spheres of interest, and to participate in the expected partition of China. Their intention was to switch the centre of gravity of Russian foreign policy to the Far East. Witte had the same ends in view, but hoped to achieve them by a peaceful understanding with China. But he was forced out of office by an unscrupulous clique of generals and speculators, who drove the country into war with Japan, and won over the weak Tsar to their cause.

The ruling circles in Russia toyed gaily with the idea of war against Japan, but gave little thought to the difficulties which the vast distances involved. The Russo-Japanese war was an unnecessary colonial war, provoked by Russia, as the Crimean War had been, but with far more catastrophic results. The military defeats which followed— the siege and fall of Port Arthur (2 January 1905), the defeat of the Russians on land at Mukden (March 1905) and the complete

142, 143 Points of view, 1904–5. *Right*, a Japanese propaganda poster. A postcard entitled 'Battle Song of the Russian Sailors' (*far right*) attempts to embarrass Admiral Togo

destruction of the Russian fleet at Tsushima (27 May 1905)—had repercussions which shook the whole Russian governmental structure. The actual territorial losses—the southern part of Sakhalin, Port Arthur, Korea and part of the Chinese Eastern railway—were not crippling. The war had been no more than a gigantic colonial adventure, which a securely based state could have carried without undue strain. But this did not apply to Russia. Lenin was right when he said that 'the fall of Port Arthur marked the beginning of the fall of autocracy'. It exposed the corruption and incompetence of the régime, as to a certain extent the Crimean War had already done. The defeats were greeted with joy by the opposition, which was preparing for a revolutionary uprising. Thus the Russo-Japanese War became what Lenin called 'the locomotive of revolution', and the revolution the locomotive for the transformation of Russia. By 1905, middle-class and aristocratic liberals, intellectuals, students and workers were ready for revolution in a way which was completely different from the state of affairs after the Crimean War. The old constitutional movement, supported largely by the nobles and the intelligentsia, had never entirely died out, in spite of the reaction. It had found congenial soil in the organs of self-government, the *zemstva*, and had taken shape as *zemstvo* liberalism. The peasants still stood mutely aside, but amongst the other elements represented in these assemblies was a reasonably powerful liberal opposition. The

so-called 'third element'—the officials appointed by the *zemstva*, such as teachers, doctors and clerks—represented a more radical wing, and a bridge to the socialists and political agitators in the countryside. In 1902 a central *zemstvo* was founded in Moscow with a view to consolidating these forces.

In addition to the liberals there were the real revolutionaries who fell into various groups. There were the remnants of the *narodniki* and of the *Narodnaya Volya*, terrorists who revived their policy of assassination; the social revolutionaries, representatives of indigenous Russian socialism, who formed themselves into a party in 1901; and finally, already growing more important, the Marxist Social Democrats. Their first organized group came into being in 1883. A Russian Social Democratic Workers' party was formed in 1898, by which time Polish, Latvian and Jewish Social Democratic parties already existed. In 1902 the periodical *Liberation* appeared, in some ways the equivalent of Herzen's *Kolokol* as an organ for pooling ideas and discussing them. On the other hand, its contents also demonstrated the continuing disunity of the left wing. Socialist and radical liberal elements were still mixed up together, and even on the Marxist wing personalities such as Plekhanov, Vera Zasulich, Martov, Axelrod and Trotsky represented different points of view regarding both the objectives of the movement, and the means by which they were to be achieved. For Marx had drawn only a broad   169 theoretical outline and it was inevitable that there should be bitter arguments about the tactics his doctrines required.

It was at this point that Lenin's full stature was revealed. With his acute dialectical mind, Lenin was a faithful follower of Marxist theory, but his actual tactics showed remarkable originality. He fought for an undivided line of action, and a unified programme which aimed to establish the supremacy of socialism through the dictatorship of the proletariat. Banished from Russia, he continued his revolutionary activity abroad with a series of short, extremely acute pamphlets, and then in his periodical *Iskra*. His disagreements with other sections of the party were bitter and led to a decisive split. This occurred at the second congress of the Russian Social Democrat party, held in Brussels and London in 1903, and led to the famous division into *Bolsheviki* (or the majority) under Lenin, and *Mensheviki* (or the minority). The questions at issue were essentially tactical. Both stood for the overthrow of Tsarism and capitalism, but the Bolsheviks wished to achieve it through the dictatorship of the proletariat. The Mensheviks, on the other hand, advocated co-operation with liberalism, the middle classes and an eventual democratic republic, and were therefore denounced by Lenin as opportunists. The struggle within the party continued for many years, but the basic split was there from 1903.

The Russo-Japanese War gave a new impetus to all the revolutionary movements. By the beginning of the twentieth century the number of those ready for revolt had grown considerably. While preparations were still being made by the different revolutionary factions, revolution broke out spontaneously as a direct result of the war against Japan.

THE FIRST REVOLUTION, THE RESTORATION AND REACTION; THE SITUATION IN 1914

The first Russian revolution took place between 1904 and 1907. A wave of strikes swept the country. In the towns there was street fighting, in the country one peasant rising followed another, and mutinies occurred in the army. Finally, the seriousness of the situation forced the régime to make increasingly substantial concessions.

144 Vladimir Ilyich Lenin

The following list of dates indicates the course of the revolution:

1904	July 28	assassination of Plehve, the Minister of the Interior
	November	first *zemstvo* congress
1904–5	December and January	street-fighting in Petersburg and Moscow
1905	January 22	'Bloody Sunday' in Petersburg
	March 3	imperial rescript providing for popular representation, but only with advisory powers
	April 30	edict of toleration
	August 19	constitution and suffrage granted in accordance with the rescript of 3 March
	October 30	the October Manifesto: a legislative Duma, to be elected by almost universal suffrage with the right to consent to all new laws; a Prime Minister (Witte) and a ministerial cabinet; the beginnings of a constitutional state. Continued concessions to the peasantry
	December	universal suffrage
1906	May 6	promulgation of basic laws and grant of a new constitution
	May 10 to July 21	meeting of the first Duma with a radical majority hostile to the régime
	July 21	dissolution of the first Duma
	July 22	Stolypin appointed Prime Minister; repression and reaction
	November 22	abolition of the *mir*
	March 5 to June 16	second Duma, equally radical and hostile to the régime
	June 16	dissolution of the second Duma and imposition of a reactionary electoral law
1907	November 14	beginning of the third Duma; conservative, nationalist and reactionary

This tabulated survey of the main events gives a clear picture of the rise and fall of the revolutionary movement, and shows how the government first made concessions and then consolidated its position. After the December revolution in Moscow, and the nomination of Stolypin as Minister of the Interior (10 May 1906) and then as Prime Minister (22 July 1906), it was clear that the revolution was not strong enough to force a break with the past. The old powers were still too resilient. The mass of the peasants could not be mobilized as a revolutionary force, and the liberals largely supported the régime, so long as it was prepared to grant concessions involving some sort of parliamentary government. The government had to accept this fact, and so as a result of the revolution Russia became a constitutional monarchy similar to Prussia. Even this was a major step forward. Moreover, the government was forced to do something about the agrarian question. The first two Dumas had made extremely radical demands in respect of agriculture. To parry these, the government made a series of concessions as a result of which the *mir* was abolished and a reorganization of the countryside became possible.

The revolution also stimulated the rise of political parties. On the liberal side there were the Constitutional Democrats, or Cadets, a middle-class party which stood for a parliamentary régime on the English model. Then there were the Octobrists, a conservative party which was content with the concessions the Tsar had made in the October Manifesto; it was primarily the party of the capitalists. On the socialist side there were three main groups, the Social Revolutionaries, the Social Democrats and the Peasants' League. None of the parties was very clearly delineated; they were still in a state of flux and as the government's power revived, it had little difficulty in withstanding party pressure.

It was not as a party, but as a means of organizing the workers that the idea of the soviet suddenly materialized during the winter of 1905. The Petersburg Workers' and Soldiers' Soviet was active from October to December 1905. The precedent was adopted elsewhere and led to the foundation of an All Russian Soviet. The principle of the soviet had no theoretical or literary preparation. It was mentioned neither in the works of Marx nor in Lenin's early

145, 146 Prime Minister Stolypin (*left*) in 1906, calm survivor of an early assassination attempt.

That summer the first Duma had been dissolved, and 'Kadets' (Constitutional Democrats) and Labour members met in the woods near Viborg, across the Finnish line (*right*)

writings. It had arisen spontaneously during the French Revolution, and in the Paris Commune of 1871. Now it reappeared as an improvisation during the strikes of 1904 and 1905. In the workers' soviets, deputies from separate factories came together; in the soldiers' soviets, representatives of the different military formations. Their purpose was to speak and act on behalf of the working class. They existed side by side with, and outside the party system. Lenin was not a member of the Soviet, just as he was not a member of the Social Democrat party in the Duma. He had not yet seen in the soviets the organ through which the dictatorship of the proletariat could be realized. For the moment his efforts were concentrated on securing a majority for his own party, and it was only when this had been achieved that he came forward with his famous declaration, 'All power to the soviets'.

The first Russian revolution was a spontaneous movement without precedent in Russian history. Its achievements were far from negligible. But it did not possess the clearly-defined liberal character of the revolution of 1848, or the clearly-defined socialist character of the November Revolution of 1916. It was stimulated by a mixture of liberalism and socialism, and was not sufficiently well prepared to achieve its ends. Though Lenin realized this, he could do nothing about it. But he appreciated the consequences and, with his remarkable tactical insight, immediately gave the order to retreat and not to return to the attack until conditions were ripe. In the mean-

time he devoted himself to the co-ordination of party tactics and the creation of a centralized, disciplined Bolshevik party.

Owing to the lack of preparation and the conflicting objectives of the revolution, the Establishment was able to reassert its power. It showed itself to be more firmly entrenched than had been assumed either at home or abroad. Nevertheless the revolution forced the government to undertake changes in internal affairs, above all in agriculture, which no reactionary measures could reverse. It also disclosed another weak point in the structure of the empire, namely the discontent among the subject nationalities. Never before had they shown their opposition to the state so firmly. From Finland to the Caucasus revolutionary nationalist movements co-operated with the Russian opposition. Their demands for autonomy, though not yet for independence, challenged the very fabric of the state. Even a Russian statesman who countenanced them was still faced with the question of how they could be reconciled with the existing centralization of the empire.

From 1906 until his assassination on 14 September 1911, Stolypin pursued a peaceful policy of restoration, reaction and nationalism—though with some reforming measures—from which his pre-war successors scarcely deviated. He restored order by repression and governed through the third Duma, which was elected on a restricted franchise, and reflected the interests of the old ruling class. Of greater significance, however, was his realization that the peasants were the most important element in the prevailing unrest; he therefore tried to wean them from revolution by introducing far-reaching agrarian reforms. His object was to create a modern structure in the countryside by abolishing the village community and giving the peasants farms of their own. In other words, a considerable proportion of the peasants were to become private proprietors. Stolypin intended his measures to favour the wealthier peasants. Those who had little land, and who, in view of the existing over-population, could not be given land, were either to move into the towns to form an industrial proletariat or emigrate to Siberia where there was land to spare. Thus he hoped to create a class of peasants owning and working their own fields, such as existed in western Europe. This, Stolypin believed, would create a conservative peasant class which would align itself with the land-owning nobility, and from which, it was hoped, the latter would derive support and strength.

This was a major project, comparable in scope and significance with the work of emancipation carried out by Alexander II. Between 1906 and the beginning of the First World War a great deal was done to put it into effect. It was to involve some 136 million *desyatini* of land (one *desyatina* equals approximately 110 acres). By 1913, work had been completed on 17 million *desyatini* and preparations were made for dealing with another 23. By the outbreak of war about twelve per cent of the project had been carried through. It was estimated that it would require forty to forty-five years in all. It is not easy to pass a final judgment on it. The socialists and the landless peasants naturally opposed the plan, which was intended to transform the peasantry into a broadly based class of capitalist farmers on the American model. Had it materialized, it would have had major consequences affecting social stratification and the revival of the economy, and would have greatly improved Russia's position on the international grain market. But for this at least one or two generations of peace were needed. In the few years between 1906 and 1914 nothing decisive could be achieved.

Although Stolypin achieved some important reforms, their effect was reduced by the increasingly reactionary policies which he himself and the third and fourth Dumas pursued. This reaction was supported by the nobility and the wealthy middle class. Although the tempo of economic and industrial progress was accelerated, discontent was still rife, especially among the industrial workers. To counteract it, the government and the Duma adopted a nationalist standpoint. They coerced the subject nationalities, including the Finns. This policy of Great Russian chauvinism had the support of the *bourgeoisie* and helped to wean it from liberalism. But in stimulating aggressive nationalism, as in other respects, the government showed an extraordinary lack of perception. It did not realize that the Russian variety of capitalism could only work in peace-time and that a war would undermine the whole structure. The Duma also surrendered to imperialism, endorsing a large-scale armaments programme and giving its support to pan-Slavism. It was an attempt to base policy on nationalism and imperialism; and in Russia, as elsewhere, it constituted a grave threat to world peace.

As heavy industry grew and became more concentrated, the cleavage between the state and the working classes became more marked. In the years immediately after 1905 the latter were disillusioned and forced on the defensive. For Lenin, in exile, the first task was to rebuild the opposition and restore morale, but he was faced by hostile elements within the ranks of the Social Democrats.

At the party conference in Prague in 1912 the Mensheviks were driven out and the Bolsheviks formed into an active, independent party. Meanwhile the deteriorating situation in Russia provided new opportunities for the socialists. The brutal suppression of unrest in the Lena goldfields in Siberia led to mass strikes in 1912. They continued on an increasing scale until 1914. There were also attempts to set up barricades in the streets. At the beginning of the First World War, conditions in Russia were critical. Dangerous internal tension prevailed when war broke out, even if the country was not in a state of collapse.

Following heavy reverses in the Russo-Japanese War, Russian foreign policy was once more centred on Europe and the Near East. Commitments in the Far East were liquidated, and agreement was reached with Japan, which ceased to be Russia's enemy. At the same time, serious efforts were made to reach an understanding with England.

The outcome was the Anglo-Russian agreement of 31 August 1907, regarding Persia, Afghanistan and Tibet. Its conclusion gave rise to a new situation, which had important implications for Germany. Other issues between England and Russia—notably Constantinople and the Dardanelles—were still unresolved, but the desire for an understanding was still there and the agreement over Asia paved the way for closer relations. This was consolidated when Edward VII visited Nicholas II at Reval on 9 June 1908. Here proposals worked out by Grey and Isvolsky regarding Macedonia were discussed. The driving force behind all this was the opposition of both powers to German policy in Turkey, symbolized by the Berlin–Baghdad railway, which was against English and Russian interests. It was an important turning-point for Russia. The hostility to England, which had existed since the Crimean War, was converted into friendship. The result was an *entente* between the two countries which was later extended by military conventions with Russia's old ally, France.

In this new situation, Germany drew closer to Austria, and the latter re-opened the Balkan question which had been dormant for more than a decade. The Austrian annexation of Bosnia and Herzegovina caused an initial crisis and nearly led to war in the spring of 1909. A second crisis arose from the Italian seizure of Tripoli in 1911. This had immediate repercussions in the Balkans, where the Christian states joined forces under the aegis of Russia to clear the Turks out of Europe. The Balkan wars of 1912 and 1913 strained international relations almost to breaking-point, for behind the local hostilities stood Russia, on the one hand, and Austria-Hungary on the other, and the latter had the backing of Germany. Hence the year which elapsed between the Peace of Bucharest (10 August 1913) and the assassination of Archduke Franz Ferdinand at Sarajevo (28 June 1914) was a fateful one. The antagonism of the great powers became more acute, and in Russia, where only a small section among the conservative ruling classes foresaw how critically war would imperil the existing system of government, influential circles became more inclined to war. The assassination of Archduke Franz Ferdinand brought on the final crisis. The Austrian ultimatum to Serbia on

147, 148 Maxim Gorky, novelist of the Revolution, was soon to make himself felt. The old guard, Chekhov and Tolstoy, are seen (*right*) in the Crimea

23 July made conflict inevitable, and because of the existing system of alliances it immediately became a general European war.

For Russia the years between 1904 and 1914 were a time of considerable material progress, but intellectually they were marked by a sterility which contrasted markedly with the activity of the last decades of the nineteenth century. The oppressive, philistine government had a crippling effect on thought and on literature, which virtually ground to a halt. The beginnings of this attitude can be detected as early as the 'eighties, and from that time on more and more people lost heart. Chekhov (1860–1904) portrayed the situation with incomparable mastery. In scenes which were characteristic of the whole period, he described the instability and emptiness of the middle classes, who had lost all capacity for constructive action. Chekhov was one of the few great literary figures of the period. Not only among the intelligentsia, but also in the field of religious thought there was a lack of creativity, the writings of Berdyaev constituting perhaps the only exception. In the background was the figure of Maxim Gorky (1868–1936), but he had not yet attained his full literary stature. Tolstoy (1828–1910) was a figure apart. His protests against the evils of the day brought him before the public eye; he was excommunicated by the Church and denounced by the government as an enemy of the state. He had already proved himself a novelist of genius, and by now he was an international figure,

149 Nicholas II, 'The Little Father', holding an ikon, blesses his troops in 1915

whose interests lay beyond the state. Both in the religious and in the ethical spheres the influence of his humanism and socialism was 'felt throughout the whole world.

A survey of the situation in 1914 would have to take account of political reaction, the constitutional monarchy—not a mere façade, but divorced from popular interests—and the prevalence of militarism, nationalism and imperialism. Other factors were the bursts of feverish financial speculation, the social tension, the moral and intellectual exhaustion of the middle classes, and above all the gulf between the rulers and the mass of the population. These were the main characteristics of Russia and the empire on the eve of war in 1914. It is impossible to judge how far disruption had progressed, how much inner strength the existing system still possessed; whether Russia, if it had remained at peace, would have experienced a new period of reform and surmounted its ills. All we can say is that the outbreak of war frustrated any such possibilities. The decision to fight was forced from the reluctant Tsar. The government also, or at least part of it, was peacefully inclined, but it was unable to control the small but insistent war party. The masses stood silently by, with little desire to fight and no hatred for other nations. Such was the mood in which Russia entered the First World War.

THE GREAT WAR AND THE REVOLUTION (1914-17)

Russia opened hostilities in August 1914, with a successful attack on East Prussia, but was quickly forced onto the defensive. The Russian advance was halted at the battle of Tannenberg (23-31 August 1914), and, as the war progressed, the Germans counter-attacked until they occupied a line running west of Petersburg roughly from Orsha to Kharkov and thence to Rostov. The German object was to divide up Russian-held territory into its alleged 'natural' components, i.e. to deprive Russia of Poland, Lithuania, the Baltic provinces, Finland and above all the Ukraine, which was then to be made dependent on Germany. The intention was to limit the Russian empire to the Great Russian territories, and to isolate it especially from the sea.

It is hard to see why this policy, which, in spite of its failure, was revived by Hitler in the Second World War, should have gained such a hold. It was based on the assumption that the German attack would unleash internal revolutions, as a result of which Russia would quickly collapse. In particular, it was assumed that the subject nationalities, including the Ukrainians, would rise in revolt in the rear of the Russian armies and thus make victory easy. In the event, they united against the aggressor, just as they had done against Charles XII and Napoleon. Furthermore, the Russian armies and economy proved far more capable of resistance than had been assumed. But they were not strong enough to fight a long-drawn-out defensive war. As time passed, the state was weakened by old deficiencies and new ones revealed by the war. There was no shortage of manpower, but the Russian armaments industry soon proved unequal to its task. Ammunition was in short supply, and the railway system broke down, making it difficult to provision the cities. In the end, this proved the insurmountable handicap.

The primary cause of the revolution was the disorganization of the economy and of communications. The situation was made more acute by the attitude of the factory workers, particularly those in the metallurgical industries, who were more numerous and better disciplined than in 1905, and who maintained contacts with the war-weary army reserves. By 1917 it was clear that the government was facing great difficulties. Even so, the upper classes did not consider a mass revolt possible. 'We were utterly unprepared for such a thing', the leader of the Cadets, Milyukov, told the French Ambassador, when circumstances ultimately led to the revolution.

The revolution broke out in St Petersburg on 12 March 1917. Workers and soldiers joined forces. Famine in the city played its part. Two hundred thousand workers went on strike. This was the 'March revolution', and it quickly spread over the whole empire. The liberal, middle-class opposition sought to use it to win power, and the situation among the workers helped them. The Bolsheviks had not yet gained the upper hand and the Mensheviks were prepared to join with the liberals in forming a democratic parliamentary government, based on a national assembly, which was to draft a constitution. Thus a provisional government actually came into existence after the abdication of the Tsar. To begin with, the middle-class liberal element under Milyukov predominated. Later the moderate socialist, Kerensky, gained ground. Both faced opposition from the workers, who were creating their own organization in the soviets, which had at once reappeared.

The programme of the provisional government was far from adequate. It attempted to side-step the demands of the peasants for more land. It thought the people would be satisfied with parliamentary government by the Duma and advocated postponing fundamental reforms until the war had ended in victory for Russia. It seriously believed that the establishment of a revolutionary government was in itself sufficient to revive the disintegrating empire and the war-weary population, and make victory possible. As Minister of War Kerensky did, in fact, launch a costly offensive between 30 June and 17 July. This policy made things easy for the opposition at home. Their programme, 'Land and Peace', was far more effective among the masses than that of the government which wanted to continue the war. The resulting quarrels occupied the entire summer of 1917. At the same time the Ukraine, Livonia, Estonia, Finland, Siberia and the Caucasian regions threw off central control, and in many towns civil war raged.

Lenin spent the war years in exile abroad, urging on his supporters by speeches and writings. His attitude was unambiguous. He desired Russia's defeat; he wanted peace without annexations and indemnities; he rejected the call to patriotism and co-operation with the liberals; he stood for undiluted socialism, for the dictatorship of the workers and peasants through a united, closely integrated Bolshevik party. He knew that these aims could not be achieved immediately and waited patiently until the other forces had played themselves out. After his return from Switzerland (16 April 1917), he gathered together the threads of the Bolshevik movement without making himself too conspicuous. His views were still widely regarded as utopian, particularly his belief that world revolution would quickly follow the seizure of power. In the soviets the Bolsheviks were still a minority.

Meanwhile, the senseless offensive at the Front, the disintegration of the army, the demonstrations and street-fighting gave added impetus to the revolution. In St Petersburg and Moscow, the Bolsheviks secured a majority in the soviets; by the end of October the party had decided upon an uprising. For his part, Kerensky made up his mind to prevent the proposed meeting of the Second Soviet Congress by force. In this way open conflict broke out between the provisional government and the Bolsheviks. On 6 November the rising in St Petersburg began, directed by Lenin from the Smolny

150, 151, 152 Early propaganda postcards (*top*) expressed a fear of phoney revolution. The demagogue in the picture is chained to a predatory capitalist. The

Institute. The following day the provisional government, which had taken refuge in the Winter Palace, was overthrown and the Russian Soviet Federated Socialist Republic was proclaimed.

At the Second Soviet Congress important decrees were at once decided upon. On 8 November a decree for the nationalization of land was promulgated, abolishing private ownership without indemnification and handing it over to the peasants. At the same session a further decree was issued declaring Russia's readiness for peace and calling on the warring nations to conclude an armistice. On 28 November a new offer was made to the Central Powers and to Bulgaria and Turkey. It was taken up by Germany, and though the

photographs show the real thing. In the winter of 1917 an official vehicle is commandeered in Petrograd, and a demonstration takes place at the Winter Palace

German terms were extraordinarily harsh, an armistice was signed at Brest-Litovsk on 17 December 1917. For Russia the war was at an end.

As early as 8 November a new government had been formed, called the Soviet of People's Commissars. Lenin was chairman, Trotsky was commissar of foreign affairs, and Stalin became people's commissar of nationalities. It was, to all appearances, an unimportant post, but the fact that it was entrusted to Stalin indicates that even at this early date the question of restoring the connection between the old European and Asiatic dependencies of the empire and the new Soviet state was in the minds of the new government.

185

Murmansk

Archangel

Dvina

Kronstadt

Leningrad (St Petersburg)

SOVIET

Sverdlovsk (Ekaterinburg)

Riga

RUSSIAN

Moscow

Niemen

Tannenberg

Orsha

WHITE RUSSIAN S.S.R.

FEDERATED

SOCIALIST

Warsaw

Brest-Litovsk

Ural

POLAND

Vistula

Kiev

Kharkov

Don

REPUBLIC

Volga

Dniester

Dnieper

UKRAINIAN S.S.R.

Rostov

TRANS-CAUCASIAN S.S.R.

0   500

Miles

153 Russia in 1923

IV THE SECOND MOSCOW PERIOD

The First World War and the Great Revolution brought the Petersburg period to an end. Events since 1917 may be said to belong to contemporary history and call for a different treatment. Our description of developments between 1917 and 1945, therefore, is only intended to illustrate how far the Bolshevik period is linked with the Russian past. The removal of the capital to Moscow was symbolic in this respect. After the long St Petersburg interlude, the old centre of Russian life was restored to its former rank. It was a conscious break with the immediate past, with Tsarism and the Russia of the Romanovs. But how far did it imply a return to the traditions of Moscow? What we have called 'the second Moscow period' provides some of the answers to this question.

FROM THE NOVEMBER REVOLUTION TO THE DEATH OF LENIN (1917-24)

The first phase in the new era of Russian history extended to Lenin's death on 21 January 1924 and to the conclusion of the so-called 'breathing space' (*peredyshka*). The most important external events in this period were the defeat of the counter-revolution and of foreign intervention, the recovery of large parts of the former empire, the restoration of peace and the conclusion of the Treaty of Rapallo with Germany in 1922. At home it was a time of privation and starvation, of civil war, 'war communism' and the creation of the Red Army, of the constitutions of 1918 and 1923, and of the 'New Economic Policy' (N.E.P.) as an instrument of pacification and economic revival. Few people in Russia or abroad believed that the Bolshevik experiment would last more than a few months. It was Lenin's great achievement to steer the country through these critical years.

Unlike the French Revolution of 1789, the November Revolution in Russia was received in Europe with a marked lack of approval or enthusiasm. In particular the new government's call for peace caused the rulers of the war-weary nations of the West much uneasiness. Nevertheless the Central Powers saw in it an opportunity to free themselves from a war on two fronts, and after long and bitter negotiations the cease-fire in December 1917 was followed by the notorious Peace of Brest-Litovsk on 3 March 1918. The Entente. on the other hand, continued the war.

From April 1918 onwards, they also began armed intervention in the Far East and Siberia, at Murmansk and in the Caucasus, in the hope of keeping Russia in the war against Germany. They were soon joined by counter-revolutionary formations led by generals of the old Imperial Army, and supported by various *émigré* organizations, which had fled abroad and were passionately agitating against Bolshevism. The struggle caused by this intervention lasted from 1918 to 1921. In the end Russia was successful, though for a time it looked as if it was on the point of disintegration.

The most serious threat to the new state came, however, from Poland, which launched an offensive in 1920, in the hope of reconquering the territories in the west of Russia which had belonged to it centuries earlier. Polish armies advanced as far as Kiev, but the Red Army, reorganized by Trotsky, counter-attacked and reached the Vistula and the outskirts of Warsaw before it was halted. Nevertheless at the Peace of Riga (March 1921) the Poles retained considerable areas of White and Little Russia, which were not won back until 1945. On the eastern front, on the other hand, the whole Far Eastern province including Vladivostock was reunited with the U.S.S.R. by 1922.

Gradually the rest of the world had come to terms with the new Russia, and from the beginning of 1921 its place in international relations was recognized. Treaties were made with Persia, Afghanistan, Turkey, Estonia, Latvia, Lithuania, Finland, Poland, England and Germany. Since it had proved impossible to overthrow Bolshevism by armed force, a policy of co-existence was now adopted. Capitalist countries were glad to trade with Russia, which was in need of imports and was still rich in natural resources, while the Soviet government welcomed trading agreements and other foreign contacts as a means of furthering the work of reconstruction.

The first years after the Revolution, until about 1922, were appallingly difficult. The Tsarist state had collapsed completely. Lenin's proclamation granting the subject nationalities of the old empire the right of self-determination hastened the process. Some of them severed their connection with Russia completely, and it looked as though the work of six centuries had been undone. With the breakdown of the old institutions, Russia seemed to be reverting to its primitive state, the cultivated land going back to wood and steppe. The economy ceased to function. There was a terrible famine in 1921, so bad as to necessitate foreign aid. The prospect of constructing a socialist state in these circumstances seemed negligible. It was nevertheless achieved.

The main outlines of the new order were established under conditions of so-called 'war communism'. The land, the forests, the rivers, all raw materials, heavy industry, the instruments of production, mines, money, communications and foreign trade were nationalized. It was, on paper, the most complete system of economic communism over a vast area that the world had ever known. But mere decrees were not sufficient to create a new system of production. Nor was it possible at first to apply the principle: 'he who does not work shall not eat', since scarcely any food was available. The starving population reacted with strikes and revolts, the most dangerous being the naval mutiny at Kronstadt in February and March 1921.

This situation forced Lenin to act. The catastrophic decline in agricultural output and the exhaustion of industry had placed the fruits of the revolution in jeopardy. 'War communism' was abandoned and its place was taken by the New Economic Policy (N.E.P.). Instead of compulsory deliveries of grain, which had led to dangerous unrest among the peasants, Lenin introduced a system of taxation in kind, and allowed the peasants to dispose of their surpluses at market prices; similar concessions were made to light industry and trade. Within the party this policy at first aroused lively opposition. But although he realized that it would necessarily mean a limited revival of capitalism, Lenin knew that it was the only way to increase production, feed the towns and revive industry. Here, as elsewhere, Lenin demonstrated his remarkable tactical sense. There is little

189

doubt that the New Economic Policy saved the Revolutionary state, which 'war communism' was on the point of destroying. But Lenin was determined from the start that it should only be a temporary phase, a 'breathing space', and he was well aware of the danger of the revival of class differences which might result. But the very first year of N.E.P. justified the experiment. Slowly at first, but surely, economic revival began.

Lenin also made great efforts to stabilize the currency and secure a favourable balance of trade. The Land Code applied the principles of the N.E.P. to agriculture, by allowing wider scope for the private economic interests of the peasants. In 1921, Lenin said: 'Ten to twenty years of good relations with the peasants, and victory on a world-wide scale is assured.' In November 1922, he spoke before the Moscow Soviet. It was his last public appearance before his fatal illness, and he used the occasion to take stock of the first five years of soviet power. Full of confidence, he assured the assembly: 'From the Russia of the N.E.P., socialist Russia will develop.'

In the meantime, despite chaos, hunger and strife, the organization of the state had been completed. A network of soviets was established throughout the land as the instruments of the proletariat and of the administration. At the Fifth Soviet Congress on 10 July 1918, the first soviet constitution was adopted. Its opening 'declaration of the rights of the working and exploited people' contained the elements of all future soviet constitutions. It was already aiming at a loose federal union for the whole of Russia. By January 1921, Soviet Russia and the Soviet Ukraine had been reunited. It was not long before they were joined by the White Russian and Trans-Caucasian republics. In 1923 the need to form a more unified body, especially for purposes of foreign policy, led to the closer federation of Great Russia, the Ukraine, White Russia and Trans-Caucasia. A state which comprised the greater part of the former Tsarist empire was again in existence; Ivan III's process of the 'reassembly of the Russian lands' was repeated.

The process of reconstruction was carried out by a party involved in acute ideological controversies, though gradually, from party congress to party congress, it was reaching greater clarity. It was due to Lenin's leadership that these controversies neither disrupted the party nor hampered Russia's revival. When Lenin died on 21 January 1924 the worst consequences of revolution and civil war had been mastered. He had created the Bolshevik party and given it, in Stalin's words, its 'most important moral possessions, its ideological content, its basic direction, its revolutionary perspectives'. 'Our doctrine', Lenin said, 'is not a dogma, but a guide to action.' He was, in fact, always a man who knew how to learn from experience. The first period in the history of Soviet Communism, the period of the construction of the new Russian state and of the revival of Russia on a Marxist basis, has therefore rightly been called the period of Leninism.

THE BUILDING OF SOCIALISM UNDER STALIN

After Lenin's death in 1924 it was some time before Stalin became undisputed master of the Soviet state. Appointed people's commissar of nationalities in 1917, he became general secretary of the party in 1922, and though this promotion recognized his abilities as an organizer, it was not intended that it should place him above the other members of the central committee of the party, among whom Trotsky was, after Lenin, the most prominent. After Lenin's death leadership passed, in fact, to a triumvirate consisting of Stalin, Zinoviev and Kamenev, and it was only at the Party Congress in December 1925 that Stalin emerged as leader. In the next three years he ruthlessly established his supreme position.

The state which Stalin inherited from Lenin was still economically and socially backward, though externally it was tolerably secure. Remnants of pre-revolutionary society still existed, and among the peasants, opposition to the revolution had not been quelled. Stalin was aware of the danger that the New Economic Policy might strengthen counter-revolutionary forces, and was determined to destroy all traces of the old class-structure both in the towns and in the countryside. Whatever opposition he encountered within the party or outside was mercilessly crushed. But it would be foolish to deny that his policy also had a constructive side. He realized that tactical manœuvring should now be replaced by the construction of a coherent socialist system. Thus began the second, or Stalinist revolution.

His basic intention was to make Russia economically independent of the capitalist countries. As he explained at the Fourteenth Party Congress in December 1925: 'The very essence and foundation of our policy is the transformation of our land from an agricultural into an industrial country which will be capable of creating its own instruments of production.' In this way the economic independence, military power, and defence of the U.S.S.R. were to be assured.

The centralized State Planning Commission now assumed responsibility for these objectives. It is not clear whether Stalin had formulated a detailed programme as early as the middle 'twenties, but at any rate he proceeded with great energy to put his aim of 'socialism in a united country' into effect. This phrase not only summarized Stalin's policy, it also mirrored the points at issue between him and Trotsky, the advocate of 'permanent revolution'. The fight with Trotskyism was not merely a personal struggle for power, but the conflict between two conceptions of what the situation required. It ended in complete victory for Stalin. First Zinoviev, then Trotsky and finally Kamenev were expelled from the party, until Stalin was left in sole control.

154, 155, 156 Two of the most famous twentieth-century Russian artists, Chagall and Kandinsky, sought to work under the Soviet régime, but both left for the West in 1922. *Above*, Chagall's *Over the Town* (1917–18), a typical evocation of his birthplace, Vitebsk. *Below*, Kandinsky's *White Background* (1920). The government favoured the less inspired style of 'social realism', of which Pimenov's *Give to Heavy Industry* (1927) is an example *(right)*

Stalin, however, still adhered to the general line of his formulated policy. This meant, above all else, an almost feverish process of industrialization. The programme was expressed by the motto 'catching up and overtaking', i.e. surpassing western Europe and the United States in industrial output. At the time both the goal which Stalin set and the methods he applied seemed utterly unrealistic; yet it remains perhaps the most original contribution of the Russian revolution to the history of our age. Its essence was planning. The first Five-Year Plan, initiated in October 1928, provided central direction for the whole constructive effort. It was, in fact, completed one year earlier in 1932, and followed by a second Five-Year Plan for 1932–7; the third was interrupted by the Second World War. These plans set out in great detail the production figures, or targets, for the periods they covered, and progress was checked throughout their operation. The labour force and the country's technical resources were stretched almost to breaking-point; the stabilization of the currency provided the necessary capital; and foreign trade, which was also essential, was controlled through state monopolies. The whole project was a combination of old and new—of modern planning and of the mercantilism and autocracy which had figured so large in earlier Russian history. Stalin shrank from nothing in mobilizing the recalcitrant population, and by harnessing all available energies for the task, he not only achieved but even exceeded the planned targets. Above all, he succeeded in changing the basic attitude to work. Work, he said, was no longer compulsory labour, as it had been in the days of capitalism, but a matter of pride and honour. By 1930, developments had reached a stage when he could announce a full-scale socialist programme. Pre-war output had been overtaken, industry had already caught up with agriculture and passed it by a short head. 'We stand', Stalin said, 'on the threshold of the transformation of our country from an agricultural into an industrial land.'

The second important aspect of the Stalinist revolution was the collectivization of agriculture. Collectivization liquidated the class-danger implicit in the New Economic Policy. It destroyed the *kulaks*, the strong individualist upper layer of the peasantry. The soil remained in public ownership but it was handed over to collective farms (*kolkhoz*). These were enormous units formed by the amalgamation of hundreds of small farms, and could in some way be regarded as a return to the tradition of the *mir* or village community. The peasants still kept their houses, gardens, farmyards and small animals as their personal property, but agriculture itself was collectivized. There were also large-scale state-farms intended to provision the towns and the army.

The new agrarian policy had profound and revolutionary effects. It ran counter to all the peasants' inherited tendencies, and was bitterly opposed. When, in 1929, it was mercilessly enforced, it caused extraordinary hardships. Millions of peasants were wiped out or deported as forced labour, and in the Ukraine and the northern Caucasus the fields were unploughed and there was indescribable famine. But by 1937, collectivism was considered complete; 93 per cent of all farms and 99 per cent of all corn-yielding areas had been brought within the system. For all the harm done, it was probably a necessary change, without which the mechanization of agriculture would have taken years to complete—if it could have been completed at all. By 1938 nearly three-quarters of the land was ploughed by tractors, and something like half the sowing and reaping was done by machines. After the agrarian chaos and the shortages of the years between 1921 and 1933, the Soviet Union was producing sufficient food; when war broke out in 1941, the provisioning of the towns and army was assured.

The revolution in industry and agriculture had social repercussions which resulted in the new constitution of 5 December 1936. This constitution marked the final abolition of the old class-system. It gave concrete expression to the system of soviets, as the foundation of political organization, and in theory at least established the equality of the different nationalities within the Soviet Union. Thus the legal and constitutional foundations of a socialist governmental structure were laid, though over all towered the party hierarchy with Stalin at its head.

There is no doubt that, by 1936, much solid constructive work had been done. At the same time the problem of external security was kept well in mind. Considerable attention was given to the Red Army and the armaments industry, and security was also the reason for the decision in 1929 to build a great new industrial centre beyond the Urals. New production plants sprang up between the Urals and Lake Baikal, based on the Altai coal deposits (in Kuznetsk and Karaganda) and the ores of Magnitogorsk. Large areas of Siberia were also opened up, and an east–west canal was constructed. These measures were intended to lead to a unified economy, covering the whole of the Soviet Union.

After the repudiation of permanent revolution and the adoption of the programme of 'socialism in a united country', resistance to the entry of the Soviet Union into the international comity of nations began to subside, notwithstanding the differences between communism and capitalism. With the rise of Hitler after 1933, relations with other countries opposed to fascism became closer, and in 1934 the Soviet Union joined the League of Nations. Stalin wanted a peaceful foreign policy, since he regarded peace as necessary to secure his aim of establishing socialism in a united country. He had little use for the idea of world revolution, and the Communist International (*Comintern*), which played a considerable rôle until about 1927, fell into the background, until it was dissolved in 1943. From the inception of the first Five-Year Plan all available forces were concentrated on completing the structure of a socialist society.

The changes which had occurred by the time the new constitution was promulgated in 1936 exercised a marked influence on the Russian people. Their attitudes, especially those of the youth, were utterly different from those of 1917. In the first place, there was a rapid growth of national consciousness. Russia was no longer a country where people lived whose soul, in Herzen's words, 'was still asleep'. Within less than a generation they had been awakened, disciplined and educated, partly as a result of a large-scale educational policy on the part of the state, partly thanks to vigorous intellectual and literary activity in the early years of the revolution. Maxim Gorky, among others, set out to create a literature which expressed the ideals of the revolution and treated the people 'not merely as the instrument of material production, but as the only inexhaustible

157 The opening of the lavishly decorated Moscow Underground in 1936 was publicized as an achievement of the régime

spring of spiritual values'. This concept of the people, and the new Russia they belonged to, gave rise to a feeling for the mother-country (*rodina*) which could lead people to dedicate their lives to it.

The new feeling of patriotism was put to a severe test by the German invasion on 22 June 1941. In the first onslaught the German troops enjoyed substantial success, and in parts of Russia there were manifestations of anti-communism which, given greater political acumen, the Germans might have exploited. In 1942, also, the initiative remained with Germany; but the long struggle for Stalingrad marked the turning-point. At the beginning of 1943, the Russians launched a counter-offensive, and kept on attacking doggedly until Germany capitulated on 8 May 1945. The vastness of the land, which had contributed to Napoleon's defeat, German underestimation of Russian powers of resistance, the technical ability of the leaders of the Red Army, the resistance of the partisans, but above all else the patriotism of ordinary Soviet citizens and soldiers in the defence of

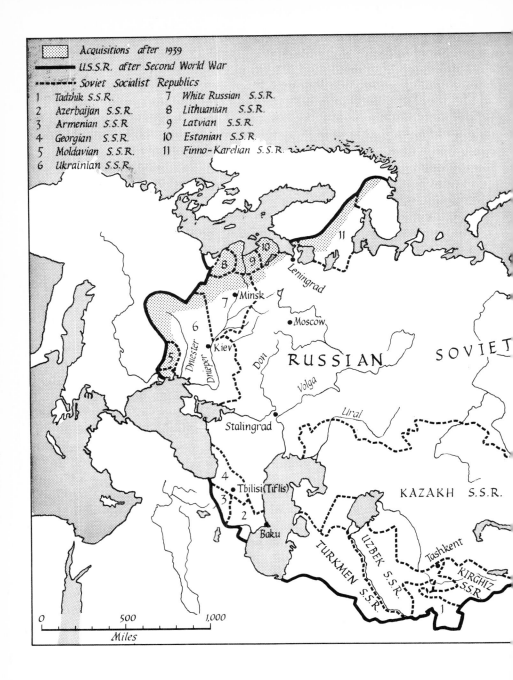

Acquisitions after 1939

U.S.S.R. after Second World War

Soviet Socialist Republics

1	Tadzhik S.S.R.	7	White Russian S.S.R.
2	Azerbaijan S.S.R.	8	Lithuanian S.S.R.
3	Armenian S.S.R.	9	Latvian S.S.R.
4	Georgian S.S.R.	10	Estonian S.S.R.
5	Moldavian S.S.R.	11	Finno~Karelian S.S.R.
6	Ukrainian S.S.R.		

11

Leningrad

8   10
9
7   Minsk
6
Kiev   Moscow
Dniester
5   Dnieper   Don   RUSSIAN   SOVIET
Volga

Ural

Stalingrad   KAZAKH S.S.R.

4
Tbilisi (Tiflis)
3
2   Baku   Tashkent
TURKMEN   UZBEK S.S.R.   KIRGHIZ
S.S.R.   S.S.R.

0   500   1,000

Miles

DERATED SOCIALIST REPUBLIC

Yenisey

Lena

Amur

Vladivostok

158 Russia after the Second World War

their homeland—all these were decisive factors. Substantial territorial gains resulted from Russia's victories. In the west it won back the White Russian and Little Russian regions which belonged to it by race and language and history, and by extending its frontiers to the Baltic, Poland and Czechoslovakia, it took over areas which it considered essential for its security.

After 1945 Russia emerged as the largest self-contained empire in the world. Its huge population and its natural resources, which have still to be fully exploited, constitute an immense potential source of energy. And yet, in spite of its revolutionary mission as a world power, the Soviet Union is still conditioned by its historical background, its centuries of evolution, which remain an active force although the context in which they work is new. Geographical factors alone, and especially the extent of Russia's territory, ensure this continuity. It is perceptible in the character of the people whose traditional qualities may have been modified, but have not been dispelled, by the revolutionary changes since 1917.

159 The Potsdam Conference, July 1945

This short introduction to the literature on Russian history is confined to books written in English or available in an English translation. It begins, as all study of Russian history must begin, with V. O. Klyuchevsky's five-volume *History of Russia* (London, 1911–31), a classic which, unfortunately badly translated, fills much the same place in Russian historiography as Macaulay, Stubbs or Trevelyan in English. Like them it is no longer up to date; but it is the starting-point from which most modern research and reinterpretation takes off. Equally important, in a different way, is another classic, *Karamzin's Memoir on Ancient and Modern Russia* (trs. Richard Pipes, Harvard, 1958).

Among the many recent general histories of Russia, George Vernadsky's (5th ed., Yale, 1954) may be singled out for mention; it has a good bibliography. B. H. Sumner, *Survey of Russian History* (2nd ed. London, 1947), is a more individual work with an established place of its own. No general book, however, is more perceptive than T. G. Masaryk's *The Spirit of Russia* (3rd imp. London, 1961): this is a work of unusual quality which has already become a classic. W. W. Weidlé, *Russia: Absent and Present* (London, 1952), is also an imaginative study.

The standard work on Russian economic development is P. I. Lyashchenko, *History of the National Economy of Russia to the 1917 Revolution* (London, 1949). For the history of the peasantry reference should be made to Jerome Blum, *Lord and Peasant in Russia from the Ninth to the Nineteenth Century* (Princeton, 1961). The description of peasant conditions in A. N. Radishchev's *A Journey from St Petersburg to Moscow*, referred to on page 105, was translated by L. Wiener (Harvard, 1958). Sir John Maynard's essays in *The Russian Peasant* (London, 1942, new ed. New York, 1962) are more elementary but sound.

The history of early Russia is dominated by the controversy between those who take a 'Scandinavian' (or 'Nordic') and those who take a 'Slavonic' view of its origins. H. Paskiewicz, *The Making of the Russian Nation* (London, 1963), examines the problems at length, but this is perhaps better left to experts. The question is also discussed by G. Vernadsky in *The Origins of Russia* (Oxford, 1959) and there is an important volume,

Kiev Rus (English trs. Moscow, 1959), by the Soviet historian B. D. Grekov. *The Russian Primary Chronicle*, the basis of written tradition, was translated by S. H. Cross (Harvard, 1930). Grekov also wrote an attractive introduction to early medieval Russian culture, entitled *The Culture of Kiev Rus* (Moscow, 1949). For the subsequent course of Russian development, and the influence of geographical factors such as rivers, R. J. Kerner, *The Urge to the Sea* (2nd ed. Berkeley, 1946), is stimulating. The impact of the Mongol invasions is the subject of another volume by G. Vernadsky, *The Mongols in Russia* (Yale, 1953).

The history of early Muscovite Russia, down to the accession of Peter the Great, can conveniently be studied in biographies. J. L. I. Fennell, *Ivan the Great of Moscow* (London, 1961), is particularly good. The life of Ivan IV, *Ivan Grozny* (English trs. Moscow, 1947), by the Soviet historian R. Wipper is also highly regarded, while Ian Grey's more recent biography, *Ivan the Terrible* (London, 1964), takes account of Soviet research. The period between Ivan and Peter the Great, the 'Time of Troubles' and the beginnings of the Romanov dynasty, is dealt with by Z. Schakovskoy, *Precursors of Peter the Great* (London, 1964).

This was the period when expansion, which was henceforward a central factor in Russian history, got under way. On this subject there is no single work to equal B. Nolde, *La formation de l'empire russe* (2 vols, Paris, 1953), but there are a large number of books on different regions and periods. Expansion in Asia is dealt with by A. Lobanov-Rostovsky, *Russia and Asia* (Ann Arbor, 1951), and D. J. Dallin, *The Rise of Russia in Asia* (Yale, 1949), but more specialized studies such as F. A. Golder, *Russian Expansion on the Pacific, 1641–1850* (Cleveland, 1914, reprinted 1960), G. A. Lensen, *The Russian Push towards Japan, 1697–1875* (Princeton, 1959) and R. A. Pierce, *Russian Central Asia, 1857–1917* (Berkeley, 1960), will also be found rewarding. Russian expansion to the south and west merges into general European history. An outline of relations with Poland will be found in R. F. Leslie, *The Polish Question* (London, 1964), and L. S. Stavrianos, *The Balkans since 1453* (New York, 1958), is indispensable. W. H. McNeill, *Europe's Steppe Frontier, 1500–1800* (Chicago, 1964), provides a stimulating account of the thrust southwards to the Crimea and the Ukraine. For the latter, the standard work is W. E. D. Allen's *The Ukraine: A History* (Cambridge, 1940), a book which avoids the exaggeration of both 'Great Russian' and Ukrainian nationalism.

With Peter the Great the modern period in Russian history begins. There is an excellent short biography of him by B. H. Sumner, *Peter the*

Great and the Emergence of Russia (London, 1951). For Catherine II, in spite of a plethora of popular lives, the position is not so satisfactory, but Gladys Scott Thomson, *Catherine the Great and the Expansion of Russia* (London, 1947), is useful as an introduction, and two important figures of the period are dealt with by B. N. Menshutkin, *Russia's Lomonossov* (Princeton, 1952), and D. M. Lang, *The First Russian Radical, Alexander Radishev* (London, 1960). A. Lobanov-Rostovsky, *Russia and Europe, 1789–1825* (Ann Arbor, 1947), covers the period of the French Revolution and the reign of Alexander I, and E. Tarlé has written the story of *Napoleon's Invasion of Russia, 1812* (London, 1942). Of Alexander I himself, as of Catherine II, there is no entirely satisfactory biography available in English, but M. Raeff's life of the Tsar's adviser, *Michael Speransky, Statesman of Imperial Russia, 1772–1839* (The Hague, 1957), covers some of the more important aspects of the reign, and Alexander's foreign policy after 1815 is placed in a European context by H. G. Schenk, *The Aftermath of the Napoleonic Wars* (London, 1947).

For the period between the death of Alexander I and the Revolution of 1917 there is an extensive literature, which is continually being added to, and only a selection of the more important titles can be given here. N. V. Riasanovsky, *Nicholas I and Official Nationality in Russia* (Berkeley, 1959), and W. E. Mosse, *Alexander II and the Modernization of Russia* (London, 1958), are standard biographies, and the history of Tsardom is continued to 1917 by H. Seton-Watson, *The Decline of Imperial Russia* (London, 1952), and Richard Charques, *The Twilight of Imperial Russia* (London, 1958). T. H. von Laue, *Sergei Witte and the Industrialization of Russia* (New York, 1963), is important for the development of industry and urbanization at the close of the nineteenth century.

But emphasis has tended to fall on the history of the intellectual and literary movements which played so distinctive a rôle after the Decembrists' revolt of 1825. *The Decembrists* themselves are discussed by M. Zetlin (New York, 1958) and by A. G. Mazour, *The First Russian Revolution* (Stanford, 1961); and there is a good account of the debate on Westernization in N. V. Riasanovsky, *Russia and the West in the Teaching of the Slavophiles* (Harvard, 1952). Among the many books on the development of radicalism and revolutionary movements F. Venturi, *Roots of Revolution* (London, 1960), is outstanding, but L. A. Haimson, *The Russian Marxists and the Origins of Bolshevism* (Harvard, 1955), and Theodore Dan, *The Origins of Bolshevism* (London, 1964), are worth consulting and B. D. Wolfe, *Three who Made a Revolution* (New York, 1948), is very readable. There are biographies of most of the leading revolutionaries, to which should be added Richard Hare, *Pioneers of Russian Social Thought* (London, 1951) and *Portraits of Russian Personalities between Reform and Revolution* (London, 1959); but there is no substitute for the writings of the reformers and revolutionaries themselves, e.g. Alexander Herzen, *My Past and Thoughts* (6 vols, London, 1924–7). For the same reason it goes without saying that no one interested in nineteenth-century Russia can dispense with the novels and plays of Gogol, Turgenev, Dostoyevsky and Chekov.

This is not the place for a full bibliography on post-revolutionary Russia and the U.S.S.R. The standard work is E. H. Carr, *A History of Soviet Russia*, of which eight volumes have appeared (London, 1950–64) carrying the story to 1926. Those who require a shorter treatment may turn to L. Schapiro, *The Communist Party of the Soviet Union* (London, 1960), or the somewhat hostile single-volume *History of Soviet Russia* by G. von Rauch (London, 1957). Maurice Dobb has surveyed *Soviet Economic Development since 1917* (5th ed. London, 1960); Richard Pipes, *The Formation of the Soviet Union* (Harvard, 1954), is an important book on Soviet nationalities policy. Christopher Hill has written a good short biography, *Lenin and the Russian Revolution* (London, 1947), and there are biographies of *Trotsky* (3 vols, London, 1954–63) and *Stalin* (London, 1949) by Isaac Deutscher.

LIST OF ILLUSTRATIONS

INDEX